TOO OLD TO HIRE
TOO YOUNG TO RETIRE

To Brian -

Thanks for all
you teachings.
I've learned much
from them.

All the best &
God bless —
Brian

TOO OLD TO HIRE
TOO YOUNG TO RETIRE

A COMPREHENSIVE GUIDE FOR
BODY, MIND, & SOUL

BRIAN HENNESSEY

Too Old to Hire, Too Young to Retire: A Comprehensive Guide for Body, Mind and Soul
Published by YAJNA PUBLICATIONS
Los Angeles, California, U.S.A.

HENNESSEY, BRIAN, Author
TO OLD TO HIRE, TOO YOUNG TO RETIRE
BRIAN HENNESSEY

Paperback: 978-0-9986163-5-3
Hardcover: 978-0-9986163-6-0
eBook: 978-0-9986163-7-7

BUSINESS & ECONOMICS / Personal Success
BODY, MIND & SPIRIT / Inspiration & Personal Growth

Book Design by Michelle M. White, www.mmwbooks.com

QUANTITY PURCHASES: Schools, companies, professional groups, clubs, and other organizations may qualify for special terms when ordering quantities of this title. For information, email brian@impactcoachingsystems.com.

Dedication

*This book is dedicated to those brave souls who
are willing to look fear in the face so it ceases to trouble them,
to discover the hero within themselves that is in each and every one
of us, and who dare to exercise their faith and courage muscles
to go after their heart's desire.*

CONTENTS

PART TWO: BUSINESS IDEAS
FOR THE NEW ECONOMY

PREFACE

At the end of 2011, I was looking for an executive real estate position as vice president of acquisitions/dispositions. After speaking with several executive search firm recruiters, I concluded that there weren't any positions open at the time. I decided to switch my search instead to a role as vice president of leasing. I found several openings, but I was told that I was not the right age they were looking for. One recruiter finally told me that I'd be better off looking at some other type of position such as property management. The recruiter said, "You're just too old to be considered an ideal candidate." I was taken aback. I never thought I'd hear those words. So, I decided to go back into commercial brokerage in 2012.

I know that this experience is not unique to me. If you're between the ages of 45 and 70, you probably have at some point felt the sting of being discriminated against for your age. Many companies want to hire the younger, less experienced, cheaper contractor, vendor, or employee.

A common lament I hear from many friends and acquaintances is, "I'm not making the same money I used to." Mostly from those who lost their jobs during the pandemic, or even as long ago as the Great Recession of 2007-2009, and have been unable to land decent work or, sometimes, any job. The industries they were in have disappeared or morphed into another form and are doing more with fewer employees by outsourcing or using part-time employees.

Like many older and experienced job seekers out there, they are frustrated, stuck, and looking for a way to get unstuck. Even those who have kept up with changing technology and have the expertise listed in the job description have a difficult time landing the job. Despite clearly being qualified, they are told they are overqualified or earn too much, code words for too old.

The one certainty in life is change, and the world is changing faster all the time. But like anything else that brings change into our lives, we can retreat and commiserate with those who don't wish to adapt to the new way of things, or we can embrace this change and figure out how to make it work for us. How we choose to respond to all of this transformation will help to determine our future course.

The one idea I put into action that changed my life in amazing ways was this: after creating a reference manual for myself about conducting due diligence when purchasing commercial properties, I placed it on Amazon to sell to investors. Sound crazy? Not really.

The decision was not exactly made without trepidation. After all, there are plenty of books available on real estate on Amazon, even back in 2012 when I uploaded the first edition. There were over 8,000 books on the subject at that time. I kept listening to my mental chatter that warned me about too many existing books on the subject already and questioned: who would read it anyway?

I finally decided it didn't matter if anyone ever read it. I was simply using it for marketing purposes. I convinced myself that it wasn't worth worrying about.

Little did I know that uploading my book onto Amazon would result in a new and unexpected role for me as a teacher. The president and CEO of the company I worked at, Colliers International, asked me to lead a webinar for commercial agents across the country. I was taken aback because I had never led a webinar before, but I accepted. The presentation was well-received. Then, I was asked to lead seminars for other offices. It snowballed from there.

I didn't realize how much I enjoyed sharing my information. The more I shared, the more proficient I became at it and the more I enjoyed it.

This one decision, which I took action on, has opened more doors for me than I ever dreamed possible. All because I allowed myself to be vulnerable. To take a chance. To not care what others think of me or my information. It's none of my business what they think.

> "... The price of inaction is far greater than the cost of a mistake. Cynics and pessimists do not change the world." – Meg Whitman, CEO, Hewlett-Packard

I went on to write two more books in the series, also putting them on Amazon. I've been an avid reader my whole life and have always remained curious about many subjects and interests. I believe in being a lifelong learner and constantly growing and improving. I find it gratifying when I receive emails from readers telling me how much the information has helped them. That really was the big payoff for me. That is what continues to drive my desire to share and help others.

Here is how this book came about. In a self-development seminar I attended, the speaker made a comment that went something like: *"I know there are many of you here today that fall into the category, "Too old to hire and too young to retire."* That phrase hit me like a ton of bricks. I loved that phrase and said to myself," *I'm going to write a book someday with that title and I know what I want it to say to help others."*

I put it in the back of my mind, but it kept coming back to haunt me. My subconscious seemed to be working on it constantly, and ideas for the book kept percolating up to my conscious mind. This went on for a few years. In the interim,

I wrote my second book. Then in 2018, I started writing the third book in my commercial real estate series. I wanted to write this hire/retire book, which I had started on. However, I knew I had to finish the commercial real estate book first, so I put hire/retire on hold. When the pandemic hit, I had the time to focus on it.

Five years ago, I decided to build additional streams of income in order to be able to retire without the stress and worry of paying the bills and with allowance for vacations and unexpected expenses. I started making more of an effort to create income streams from my online courses, books, and audiobooks, and I ramped up my coaching and consulting businesses.

During the course of learning the essential skills needed to create these income streams, I attended a number of classes and seminars, read and listened to hundreds of books, and watched dozens of webinars, YouTube lessons, and video courses. Some were life altering and catalysts for how I began viewing business and the world at large. I'm grateful that it has paid off, and I'm happy to share my experience. My objective here is to offer you a paradigm shift—a new way to look at the opportunities and possibilities that are available in today's world. This will require you to be open-minded while reading or listening to this book. If you allow yourself that option, you will be pleasantly surprised by how many possibilities are open to you. Not only will you be able to create a nice lifestyle for yourself now, but you can even retire with a much better lifestyle than you thought possible.

I have also been a daily meditator for over 35 years. I credit my spiritual training and discipline with helping me to obtain the accomplishments and achievements that I have made.

I've been blessed throughout my life with great mentors and people who love me. I have a loving wife who is my best friend and two great kids. I've survived lung cancer and enjoy good health. I want to continue to serve God by serving others in every way possible. If I can help one other person with the information and ideas in this book, it will have been well worth all my efforts.

I relate these stories and my experiences to you, dear reader, not to boast about my accomplishments, but to show you that you don't know what is possible until you step outside your comfort zone and take some risks. It can be one decision you take action on, even one that scares you, that will be a major game changer for you. By doing so, you are already way ahead of the vast majority who remain well within their comfort zone, unwilling to take any chances.

The essential skills and lessons I discuss in the book are based upon my experience. My desire is to share these with others who want to get ahead and improve their lives. These suggestions work. You just have to be open and willing to apply yourself and work them.

If I can do it, you certainly can. There are two ways to learn: through your own mistakes or from others'. It's always easier, quicker, and cheaper to learn from others' mistakes. I've made plenty of mistakes in my life. Many of the lessons in this book were learned from my mistakes. You don't have to make them too. Shorten your learning curve and learn from mine.

By the way, that's how we humans learn. By trial and error. Don't be afraid of making mistakes or failing. It's only failure if you don't learn from it. Just go out there, have fun, and enjoy the journey.

This book will give you a road map, offering you plenty of ideas, inspiration, strategies, resources, and tips (the tips are numbered throughout, so you can make note of the ones that are of interest and return to them later, if you so desire). Also, there are step-by-step instructions for what you can and need to do in order to get moving in a positive direction. At the ends of most chapters, there is a list of 'Action Items' so you can get started immediately on those ideas and strategies that resonate with you.

Don't break down; break *out* of the old way of thinking. If you're not willing to spend the time, energy, and effort to help yourself, who will? The one person you can count on, with certainty, is yourself. Because that's all you truly have control over and because you have the skill, the talent, the determination, and the ability to design your own route to your goals and objectives.

The good news is that there are more opportunities and options available to us today to not only survive but *thrive* than ever before. That's what this book is all about.

It's never too late to learn to become your best self. You can be your own greatest enemy, or your own best friend. It's your choice.

So, let's get started with getting your mindset trained and opened to seeing the opportunities ahead instead of obstacles while losing the stress and worry about your future.

Remember, just one idea *put into action* can change your entire world just like it did for me.

Brian Hennessey

Brian Hennessey

INTRODUCTION

———

Congrats! You've taken the first step on your new journey to turn your world around by taking control of your own future. That first step is a major one because too many people become paralyzed with fear and are unable to move forward.

This book is jam-packed with plenty of ideas, tips, strategies, and resources for you to get started and catapult your life into unlimited possibilities.

After taking a break from my yoga classes due to some health issues, I went by the studio only to see it was shut down. I gave my instructor, Mahnaz, a call and asked her where the new studio was located. She said, "There is no new studio. I shut this one down and my new studio downtown as well. Too many others have opened up in the area, and I can't make it with the number of students I had of late. So, I shut both locations down. Now, I'm trying to figure out what to do to earn a living."

I was taken aback because she had a good following and is an excellent teacher. I asked her to meet me for coffee and to discuss her options. She was noticeably down, which is not her personality. She's generally a very upbeat and positive person. I told her she had too much to offer to not continue her yoga instruction. I suggested she write a book. At first, she dismissed it as not for her. There were too many books out on yoga and the market was flooded with information about it. I then explained that it wasn't about that. I told her it's about the way you teach it and your voice and techniques. You just need to be yourself and let your own passion shine through.

She started to see what I was telling her and began asking me questions about where to start. I told her she needed to write the book that she would want to read about her story and exactly how she does what she does best. For her, that is teaching others the style of yoga she has taught for many years, which many other students benefited from, including me. We talked for a bit as I explained how to go about organizing her thoughts, creating an outline and a table of contents, and starting to break it down as she crystallized her thoughts about what she wanted to say.

We talked again over the next 3-4 months as she progressed with her book. In the meantime, the pandemic hit. I suggested she restart her yoga classes online, which she did. As the weeks rolled on, her classes were adding more people. Things began to progress, and she is now working on her online course materials. She essentially re-engineered the way her business was running and headed into the new economy with more hope and promise. She has many more ideas as to how she wants to create new streams of income from her business. She is creating yoga retreats and other events that she wants to offer when things open back up. And yes, she finished her book and is selling it on Amazon.

I relate this story about Mahnaz so that you can see how individuals can turn their worlds around simply by adjusting their attitudes and approaches.

Believe

First, and most importantly, keep an open mind and allow yourself to imagine achieving your objectives and goals. Instead of, "I'll believe it when I see it," think, "I'll see it when I believe it." You must start believing it's possible. It may seem far out there, but that doesn't mean it's not possible. Anything is possible if you believe. *Start believing.* That's your first step.

Action

The next important step is to *get into action.* Even if it's something as simple as writing down your next action steps and taking one action toward your objective. Each time you take an action it helps to program your mind and body to act again. You can start out small and build on your actions each day. Just make sure you do something *each day.* If you do, you'll find that it will build upon each previous action and become stronger, until it becomes as natural to you as brushing your teeth.

Schedule and Track

Get yourself a calendar, and schedule and plan your day to include the steps you will take. Make yourself a priority, and block this time off. To track your progress, mark off each day that you take an action, so you have a visible reminder that shows you the progress you're making daily.

Positive Messaging

An essential habit to incorporate into your daily routine is to read or listen to positive messaging for at least 20-30 minutes, first thing in the morning, before you start your day. Do it while drinking your coffee or tea when your mind is fresh and open to new ideas and messages to direct your thinking for the day ahead. Think of it as mental vitamins for your brain. There are plenty of helpful resources listed in the back of the book. You'll see a major positive change in yourself once you establish this habit.

Get Started

To jump-start your new adventure, there is a list of suggested action items at the end of almost every chapter. After reading each chapter, I highly recommend you implement at least one of the action items, so that by the time you reach the end of this book, you will have started your new journey with many tools in your 'toolkit' to help propel you along the way.

TIP 1: Ideas are fleeting. They will escape if you don't capture them. Take notes while reading through this book, so you'll have your ideas and thoughts written down for future reference. If you're listening to this as an audiobook, have a recorder ready or use the one on your mobile phone, so you can stop and record your ideas on what you just heard. Or, write them down in a notebook or on your phone or computer. Review them within 24 hours. For the next seven days, review again daily for at least 10 minutes. Your recall will increase dramatically to about 80%.

Listening to audiobooks is one of the fastest ways to obtain great information you can use to supercharge your life in a short period. I listen to audiobooks constantly when driving, walking, exercising, or even doing chores. After I finish a book, I'll transcribe my recorded notes into a notebook for later review. Then, I'll add my thoughts as to how I can apply the ideas I've collected. I've been able to capture and use many terrific strategies, tips, and suggestions in my own life and work.

If you're only listening to music, talk-radio, or sports, you're missing out. It's basically chewing gum for the mind. I'm not saying you should never again listen to them. What I'm saying is that you should limit the amount of time you spend on those categories and instead listen more to books, podcasts, and information that will enhance your abilities to move closer to your objectives and enrich your life.

If you make this one of your new habits and listen to at least two books each month, you'll have completed 24 books in a year and can catapult your knowledge in any area you choose. There are a number of ways to access audiobooks including Audible.com, Google Play, Audiobooks.com, and free library apps like OverDrive and Cloud Library. If you haven't listened to audiobooks in a while, you'll find that they have improved and are easier to listen to than they were years ago. More people have turned to them instead of reading.

In addition, there are many outstanding podcasts you can subscribe to on just about any subject you're interested in. Sample some of these until you discover the ones that resonate with you. The great thing is that you can listen to them whenever you find the time.

YouTube is another excellent educational resource. There are many YouTube channels where you can pick up new information and learn new skills.

TIP 2: What I do that allows me to listen to more audiobooks is to set my Audible app player listening speed setting to 1.5X to 1.8X. It plays the recording a little faster, but it's still easily understood. I'm so used to it now that it sounds too slow when I switch it to normal speed.

There are multiple resources available to help you learn new skills and acquire the knowledge you need to take your life and your world to a new level. It's all there for the taking. I recommend many throughout the book and in a special section at the end. I have no business compensation with any of them, and I do not receive any referral income or services for listing them; I just want to share them as valuable options. You just need to make the decision to do whatever it takes to turn your life into the one you want it to be. Make up your mind and get into action.

I also include throughout the book some inspirational words for the spiritual aspects of life. As I discovered in my life, the spiritual portion of it is part of the whole. Without addressing that aspect of yourself, you'll not only feel like something is always missing, but you'll also be missing out on a key component for true all-around success. Success should be measured by the yardstick of happiness. I share my beliefs and faith in the hopes that you, dear reader, may benefit in some of the ways I have from them.

ACTION ITEMS

✔ Sign up for a library app or an audiobook provider like Audible.com, one of the best learning tools and bargains out there.

✔ To begin your reading habit, choose 2–3 books that meet your specific needs and interests. Topics might revolve around your mindset, occupation, or some activity you are thinking of exploring for monetary or personal growth reasons, etc. Build a wish list on Audible.com of several books that you can look forward to listening to.

✔ Decide when you'll listen to these audiobooks. Perhaps while driving or commuting to work, exercising or walking the dog, doing work around the house, or running errands.

✔ Read for one hour daily. That can be 20–30 minutes at different times of the day. Schedule the time(s) to sit down and read uninterruptedly. Morning is a great time to read self-improvement/motivational/inspirational books to launch your day on a positive note.

✔ Check out YouTube for information on how to generate additional income. Many great YouTube channels provide terrific information for free.

PART ONE

ESSENTIAL STRATEGIES, HABITS, AND SKILLS FOR THE NEW ECONOMY

Chapter 1

TIME FOR A PARADIGM SHIFT

When discussing with others their frustrations with their current occupations or lack of choices available, I often ask why they can't come up with other potential lines of work that they could explore or even create for themselves.

A typical answer is usually something like, "This is all I've done for the past 15, 20, or 35+ years. It's all changing or going away, and my skillsets are based upon this industry/ business."

I totally get that. But, there are parts, if not all, of those skillsets that you have that are valuable and can be ap-

"How long can you afford to put off who you really want to be? Your nobler self cannot wait any longer. Decide to be extraordinary and do what you need to do—now."

– Epictetus

plied in other ways to help others. One approach is to package that knowledge to be instructional and taught so that others can benefit.

My good friend, Jerry I. shares his story:

"In my job search I found myself interviewing for a position as a drywall estimator for a local company where I thought I was a shoe-in until the business owner asked my age. Shocked, to say the least, and knowing that in California a prospective employer is not to ask such a question, I went ahead anyway and replied, 44. That pretty much ended the interview as I was told that many younger individuals had applied for the same position.

"I started thinking about what else I could do. With a history of writing business plans and originating commercial real estate loans, I capitalized on my experience and began traveling internationally again and this time I was conducting due diligence on various commercial real estate projects. Later, I thought about it, and why not? I found myself eligible and studied for a few months and passed the CFE exam, becoming a Certified Fraud Examiner. After several months having no success with my attempts to work with churches and their fraud related problems, I met Brian Hennessey, the author of this book, who encouraged me to write a book of my own about business and commercial real estate fraud. I jumped right on it, taking eight months to write my own book. With the book completed, I was now looked upon with credibility in the field of fraud and commercial real estate.

To sum up my experiences, both successes and failures, I never gave up and owe it all to prayer and to the people I surrounded myself with. I looked for and took advantage of opportunities that came my way by continually preparing myself, learning new things, networking, meeting new people, and never looking back. Sure, there were and always will be tough times, and people like the drywall guy who told me I was too old will always exist. However, dwelling on the negative or giving up was never an option. Sure, I felt bad at the time, but rather than addressing a no-win situation, I saw it as an opportunity to find something better. I pray and remind myself daily that winners never quit, and quitters never win."

Jerry didn't sit around feeling sorry for himself. He picked himself up and figured out a new direction based on his skills.

Let me explain how this can work. Let's say you've been an insurance agent for 20-30 years and have seen your territory diminished as well as your commissions. You're feeling burnt out and tired of having to answer to your supervisor as to why you were unable to hit your production goals again. Business development seems to become more and more difficult as the years progress. You used to be able to make a good living and provide for your family. It has become a much tougher row to hoe than it once was. But that doesn't mean your knowledge and value are any less.

As an insurance agent, you developed certain skills through-out your career that made you effective and successful. This expertise can now be used in a different way. Here are some ideas that come to mind:

- Navigating the insurance choices available to consumers and businesses
- How to make sure you're properly covered by your insurance
- How to shop for the right insurance policy
- Factors that should be considered when picking an insurance company
- Enlightening consumers and companies about other insurance-related factors they must consider

Basically, you become a consultant in your industry for the end user. You educate your clients without the pressure of a sale looming over them. It takes away all the concern from them feeling like they're being sold.

That is what consumers want today. That want to be educated and advised about what they're looking to buy, invest in, or sign up for. They don't want to be sold. Nobody really likes that.

Next, people will usually ask, "How do you go about becoming a consultant?"

The best way is to write a book about your tips and strategies that can help others with whatever skillset or knowledge you possess. I'm not talking about a 250-page tome of information. Most people will not even consider looking at something like that. What I'm talking about is an 80-150 page book that summarizes what you're trying to impart to them. Sure, it could go a bit longer as long as you don't make it a 250 to 350-page volume.

This information may not necessarily give them all they need to know, but it will give them a firm foundation to work from. It can also be a door opener for you for further consulting.

The self-publishing industry has exploded in recent years. It's easier than ever to get your book up on Amazon or some other platform and out there for the world to see. There are countless websites with information about self-publishing. You should also take advantage of freelance editors and designers to create a book that is professional and polished. I have a great book editor and designer, Michelle M. White, who I enjoy working with and has helped me tremendously. I have her contact information at the back of the book under Resources, should you have an interest in using her services for your book. In addition, I've used editor Sophia Fischer, who has also been a big help. Her contact info is also located there.

Once you a have a book on your subject, your credibility goes way up. People automatically assume you must be an expert in your field if you've written a book on your subject. The fact of the matter is that you are more knowledgeable than most people out there looking for information on your subject. If you can offer a practical guide and help for others to make informed and intelligent decisions on that subject, then you are offering them something of value that will be appreciated.

I speak from experience. This consultant approach has helped me immensely. I've worked in commercial real estate for over 35 years and several years ago began to write books related to the industry. As a result, doors opened for me that might not have had I not written those books.

It doesn't matter what your field of expertise is or the number of years spent in that occupation. In fact, it doesn't even have to be many years at all. The idea is to think about how you can use your own experience to bring value to someone else.

This is not a new concept but one that can be profitable. There are teenagers who have written instructional book-lets that teach skateboarding tricks and grandmothers that demonstrate how to make parrot diapers. Their know-how is making them six figures. The list goes on and on with ex-amples of others who are sharing their knowledge.

TIP 3: You can springboard off your book with other additional products that can become multiple streams of income.

- You can create an audiobook from it. No, you don't have to record it yourself. You can hire someone off upwork.com, freelancer.com or some other website that connects you to independent voiceover ac-tors who can bid to record your audiobook. Most will also upload it to Audible.com, so you don't even have to do that.
- You may even want to create a video course on your subject and sell that. I'll talk more about that later in the book. You can record from your computer or even your smartphone. I suggest having it edited by an independent freelance video editor from one of the aforementioned or other websites. The result will be much more professional and can be done inexpensively. You can then upload it or have it uploaded to Udemy, Creative Live, or any number of sites that host courses. It can potentially bring in a nice income stream.
- The other big advantage you may be able to derive from your exper-tise is consulting. If your information is well-received, there will be people out there willing to pay you for your knowledge. Nothing is quite like getting personalized instruction on a desired subject.

Here is Where a Paradigm Shift May Be Needed

I often hear people say, "Well that's great for you and some others, but I know there's a ton of information on my field of expertise out there. The last thing that is needed is more information from me."

You must realize that *your voice* is different from that of others whose information is out there. It doesn't matter how much is out there or who else has information on your subject available. People are attracted to and learn from others who have a way of explaining and teaching things that resonate with them.

TIP 4: You just need to find out who "Your 1000 True Fans" are. There's an article of the same name from Wired magazine's Senior Editor, Kevin Kelly, that has become a classic in the internet marketing field. It's a must read. Tim Ferriss, author of *"The Four-Hour Work Week"* credits the article for changing his mindset.

Essentially, it states that once you've identified your 1000 true fans, further momentum is created. That's because those fans go on to tell two people, who tell two people, and so forth. This exponentially builds your fan base and more awareness and momentum.

It all starts with *believing*. You must believe that your information is helpful to others. The funny thing about human nature is that we tend to over-value others' opinions and under-value our own. First, you MUST believe in yourself. How can you expect others to believe in you if you don't believe in yourself?

TIP 5: Your information can help add value to others. If you need further proof, offer your services and information for free at first. Ask for feedback on how your services were beneficial. Then after you've helped them some, ask them if they think that what you're offering them is helpful. If they say "Yes," then tell them you'll give them a discount on your services if they'd like further help from you.

It is sometimes said that all we need is someone who believes in us more than we do to give us a push to get started. There's a strange truth to that.

I remember the first time I received an email from someone thanking me for sharing my information and how much it helped them. It was such a gratifying feeling. It's hard to explain, but it demonstrated to me that a big payoff existed for sharing my expertise.

I can promise you that when you receive your first email telling you how much your information helped someone, you'll be amazed how it affects you in a positive way. It had a big impact on me, and it is one of the driving reasons I continue to want to help others.

Perhaps you still aren't sure of what you should be looking to do next. I know how you feel. I felt the same way. But what I've found is that it may take time and soul searching before you discover what direction you should be heading in or what your true purpose is. Part of that journey may be some trial and error efforts at different endeavors before you stumble upon what's right for you.

It's a process that is well worth the effort to go through. Keep in mind that you need to align your values, strengths, gifts, and talents. It takes time to think through it to determine what those are. Really dig deep to figure out what it is that you feel would make you truly happy to be doing. Does that mean you'll be ecstatic all the time once you do? No, but you'll feel happier, more on track in your life, and more aligned with your true purpose.

Let me finish off this chapter by saying it's time for you to start thinking of the possibilities you can create with your skillsets. Spend time thinking about the different ways you can do that. I'll talk later in the book about ideas for brainstorming and exercising your creative mind muscles. We all have them; we just need to stimulate them more.

ACTION ITEMS

✔ Take alone time to begin thinking about how you can
use your expertise to help others.

✔ Create a list of 20 things you're skilled or talented at
doing, not only in your occupation or previous jobs but
whatever you're naturally good at. It doesn't matter
what it is. Get a blank piece of paper and write at the
top: 20 Things I am Good At. Give yourself one hour
to complete it. Don't prejudge anything that comes to
mind. Just put it down in writing and don't stop until
you have 20. You can add more ideas if they come up.
What you'll find is the first 5-10 things come up easy,
but the next 3-5 are tough, and after that it can be
extremely tough. But that is where you can generate
some of your best ideas. Remember, don't stop until
you have at least 20.

✔ Review the list and choose one idea that you think
would be the best one to start with. Now, create a new
list of skills that come under that specific area that you
can help others with. If that one idea doesn't flow as
easily as you thought it might, try the next one. What
you're trying to do is find the one that most naturally
flows and resonates with you. Most importantly, just
get started and take at least one action on your list.
It's much easier to develop ideas from those where
your strongest interests are.

Chapter 2

MIND MAPPING YOUR WAY TO YOUR NEXT STEPS

Mind mapping is a highly effective way of transferring information in and out of your brain. It is a creative and logical means of note-taking and note-making that literally maps out your ideas.

One simple way to understand a mind map is to compare it with a city map. The city center represents the main idea. The primary roads leading from the center represent the key thoughts in your thinking process and the secondary roads or branches represent your secondary thoughts, and so on. Special images or shapes can represent landmarks of interest or particularly relevant ideas.

> *"To think is easy. To act is hard. But the hardest thing in the world is to act in accordance with your thinking."*
>
> – Johann Wolfgang von Goethe

The terrific thing about mind mapping is that you can put your ideas down in any order, as soon as they pop into your head. You are not constrained by thinking in any particular method. The goal is to pull all of those ideas out. You can organize them later.

For those of you unfamiliar with mind mapping, let me explain how it works, and what a fantastic way it is to generate ideas and brainstorm projects.

Essentially, you start with your main subject or idea in the center of a circle on a paper or computer. Then draw a line from the edge of the circle and write another aspect of the subject. You continue doing that with each new idea or aspect of the main subject. When other ideas come up that are related to ones you've already put down, simply attach a line with another circle on it to the idea that it's relevant to. For a visual of what mind mapping can look like, I've included links in Tip 6 below to several online mind mapping sites.

For example:

- Think of your general main theme and write that down in the center of the page, e.g, Income Producing Ideas.
- Figure out sub-themes of your main concept and draw branches to them from the center. Your page will begin to look like a spider web, e.g., Skills I Possess; Knowledge I can Share; Ways I can Help Others; Hobbies I have that I can Monetize, etc.
- Make sure to use very short phrases or even single words.
- Add images to invoke thought or get the message across more clearly.
- Try to think of at least two main points for each sub-theme you've created and construct additional branches.

TIP 6: Another option is to utilize an online mapping software program. There are some great mind mapping programs out there that make the process even more fun and interesting. Google mind mapping and you'll discover several programs and articles. Some are very basic, and others can be comprehensive, allowing for exploration and brainstorming of complex subjects, ideas, and problems. Check out the following free mind mapping software programs: clickup.com, mindmup.com and mural.co.

I've used the mind mapping concept both ways, written and online. I still like drawing it out on a sheet of paper or a sketch pad that allows for more room to be used. I sometimes use various colored pens or markers to differentiate the ideas and sub-ideas. The online mind mapping programs also have fun built-in colors and images as well as hyperlinks and other features you can build into them.

Once you've had a chance to play around with either mind mapping option, you'll find it to be a productive process to generate new ideas and solutions for problems, challenges, tasks, projects and anything else that requires organizing your thoughts. Give it a try and see for yourself.

SAMPLE MIND MAP

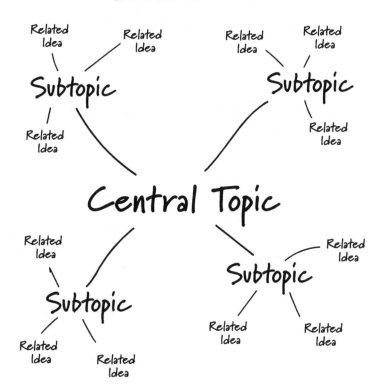

ACTION ITEMS

✔ Check out YouTube videos that demonstrate how mind mapping works.

✔ Obtain an audiobook or book on mind mapping.

✔ Test the two different mind mapping processes to learn which one works best for you. Generate new ideas and structure them.

Chapter 3

HOW TO GET YOURSELF UNSTUCK

The world has changed dramatically since the coronavirus pandemic and will continue to evolve even more quickly with the accelerated technological advances we constantly have. Essentially, it turned our world and its economies on its head, testing all our resources: physically, mentally, and spiritually. I made the decision when it happened to turn it into a positive event in my life and to strengthen as well as transform myself in all those areas.

"Your success and happiness lie in you. Resolve to keep happy, and your joy and you shall form an invincible host against difficulties."
– Helen Keller

I observed members of my family, friends, acquaintances, and others whose reactions to such a calamitous event varied immensely. As time went on, I saw that those who made a conscious effort to adopt a positive attitude were faring much better than those who were perennially negative and constantly watching all the bad news being doled out, as if it were the only reality of the situation. They felt and were acting as helpless victims of this catastrophic event. Then there were others content to binge watch Netflix or whatever else was their distraction of choice. These are not the most constructive of choices, but some folks prefer to escape.

The one thing we do have control of in life is our attitude. Ultimately, that will determine how we handle the tests and the vicissitudes that life brings us.

The new economy comes with a host of opportunities for us to learn from and to grow as individuals. There will be those who don't choose to see it that way. Unfortunately for them, it will be a very difficult path to follow.

One of the most important decisions we can make is to do our best to remain positive, even when things are at their most difficult. Exercising our courage and faith muscles is a necessity if we are to thrive and not just survive. That means we must be in action and act as if things will turn out fine if we just maintain the right attitude and efforts. Because they will.

God is the provider, not us. But we must do our part. Believe that. Know that.

Using our will power opens the way for our prayers and efforts to come to fruition. If we ask God for guidance with faith, He will show us the way to make it happen even if we make mistakes. That means we must fully believe that it will happen. You can't say, "It's going to happen," and then say or think to yourself, "I sure hope it all works out. If it doesn't, I'll be in the street and homeless," and continue to worry about it.

Our faith, patience, and courage will be tested during trying times. That's exactly when we should build these qualities up and make them stronger and more resilient.

I know from my own life experiences that when those tests come, you must make up your mind that you will overcome anything that is thrown at you, as long as your faith is strong. Sometimes it seems like it may never end, or your efforts are not coming to fruition. Stay strong and you will see that God does come through. Sometimes it seems as though it miraculously comes when you least expected it.

One thing we need to remember is that God doesn't always give us what we want, but He gives us what we need for us to grow.

As it states in the Bible, *"As you believe, so shall it be done unto you."* This is according to the degree of your faith.

These are lessons in life we are presented with. Unless and until we make the conscious decision that we will do what's necessary to move forward with a positive mindset and take on the tasks we're faced with in order to progress, we'll continue to think like victims.

There are plenty of opportunities out there, more than we ever had before. Our task is to find the ones that resonate with us. The ones that fit our skillset or we feel a natural inclination towards. Then, put the *Law of Action* into effect. This universal law is necessary for things to happen. We need to do our part by working toward our objectives, whatever they may be. This is demonstrating your faith.

For those of you who are not familiar with the term "universal law", they are those natural laws set into action which are inexorable, like gravity. You don't have to believe for them to work. They work regardless of your belief in them. You jump off a building, you will hit the ground every time, whether you believe in gravity or not.

One thing I can't help you with is getting into action. It's not enough to read about this stuff. We all have purchased books, audio programs, and video courses and even attended expensive seminars and programs, only to get fired up and then do nothing with the information.

I know because I've been there. I have benefitted greatly from some of the information and training I've received. But, I also know I never implemented some of the information I paid for despite investing time, money, and energy.

I'm not saying that all of the ideas here are going to resonate with you. However, I can say with certainty that if you don't act on the information, you will not see any benefit.

You can't just sit there and wait for success to fall into your lap. Once your course is set and your will is firm, you must make a practical effort!

Inaction breeds doubt and fear; ACTION breeds confidence and courage!

It's easy to become paralyzed with self-doubt and discouragement. They are the two of the most common and insidious of mental obstacles. These are self-defeating habits you must overcome. They will keep you from even attempting to begin!

TIP 7: One thing I've found about taking action is that you start to receive feedback and direction on what is and isn't working. This feedback helps to build momentum and brings results much faster. It's the one common denominator of all great achievers: being highly action oriented.

Stop holding yourself back. Don't worry about looking foolish, making mistakes, or failing. Failure is just feedback anyway.

Failure and success are interrelated. You don't have one without the other. It's only failure when you stop trying. The rest of the time you're learning about what doesn't work.

Most people spend way too much time trying to figure out everything before they even get started. It's ok to think through your idea, but don't get stuck by analysis paralysis. That's when people can't get out of their own way to make a decision and move forward.

In Silicon Valley, people are judged by the number of times they have failed at projects. If they have a low failure rate it is looked upon unfavorably. That sends the message that they are either afraid of failure or they just haven't gotten into action much. Failure is worn like a badge of honor there.

All of the great technology entrepreneurs experienced numerous business failures before finding success, including

Steve Jobs, Steve Wozniak, Elon Musk, Larry Ellison, and Mark Zuckerberg. When you read their biographies, it becomes apparent that they all underwent many tests of failure and disappointments before reaching their goals. There are no easy buttons to push to get there.

If you're having difficulty breaking free from the inertia, start by taking small first steps and then build upon those actions. Most often, you'll find that small steps will be enough to get your momentum moving.

We've all felt stuck at times in our lives. There's nothing wrong with that. What's wrong is not doing anything to get yourself unstuck.

I feel for those who are dealing with mental obstacles that have left them feeling helpless and paralyzed. It can be compounded by depression, anxiety, and other issues that only make things worse like drug and alcohol dependency. If you are facing anything like that and are unable to break loose from its grip, then you must seek professional help.

Most of us are trying to figure out our next steps to move forward once we decide to make things better for ourselves.

There's always a way out of our troubles and situations. We have to make up our minds that we're going to figure it out. We need to exercise those flabby courage and faith muscles that have been unused for some time. It's true that God does help those who help themselves. Prove it to yourself. I've proven it to myself over and over. You must have more faith in yourself. Remember, it's all feedback! It's only failure if you give up!

Worry, fear, and discouragement only add to the weight of our daily burdens; cheerfulness, optimism, and will power are what bring about resolutions to our problems. Worry is simply negative goal setting.

Whatever your faith or religion may be, you can tap into it in a greater way to find strength in times of difficulty. Prayer is very powerful and most of us don't realize the power it contains simply because we haven't tried it.

This is how it works:

Ask, believe, receive. It's that simple. But you must do your part.

I offer you these quotes, which have given me encouragement and solace through many challenges, from Paramahansa Yogananda, author of the spiritual classic *Autobiography of a Yogi*.

> *Remain calm.*
> *Do your best.*
> *Leave the rest to God.*
> *That is all He expects.*

> *"You must first thoroughly believe in your own plans and then let the Infinite work through you. You must do your best, but at the same time FULLY BELIEVE that God is helping you. You must realize the power of your own consciousness."*

> *"Draw on God for the solution to all your problems. Do not allow your courage and quick wit to be paralyzed when overwhelming difficulties suddenly come down on you like an avalanche. Keep awake your intuitive common sense and your faith in God and try to find even the slenderest means of escape, and you will find that means. All will come out right in the end, for God has hidden His goodness behind the superficiality of the paradoxes of mortal experiences."*

ACTION ITEMS

✔ Make up your mind that you're going to make a supreme effort to become the person you want to become and need to become in order to achieve those goals and objectives you set for yourself.

✔ Decide today that you are going to get into action mode, and then take one active step to get yourself moving in the direction you want and away from being unstuck. That can be as simple as making a to-do list of the items you're going to work on. Then take one item from that list and do it. After that, do another one and start building momentum. Make sure you make it a daily habit.

✔ Start building daily habits that help strengthen you physically, mentally, and spiritually. You'll find that as you build on your habits, you'll become more confident and positive about the progress you're making. That will keep you motivated and moving in the right direction.

Chapter 4

VISION WITHOUT EXECUTION IS FANTASY

We need to have a vision of what we want to accomplish and what it will look and feel like when we get there. Of course, it's an ongoing process that is continuously changing and morphing as we progress. However, we must create a target vision to give us a goal or objective to work toward. Developing a vision also requires us to think through the processes we need to create in order to get there. Yes, it will be a work in progress that we'll be constantly tweaking and re-engineering as we continue our visionary path. That's part of what it takes to make things happen. If we stay flexible and adaptive, we can get there. It may not look exactly as we originally saw it, but we must trust and have faith that we will reach our goal the way we are meant to.

What gets measured gets done; what gets measured and fed back gets done well; what gets rewarded gets repeated.
- John E. Jones III

Many of us are visual learners. We think in pictures. Your vision is your mind's picture of the person you will someday be and the life you'll create. That concept consists of a series of smaller goals and objectives that you are reaching for and achieving one step at a time.

TIP 8: Jack Canfield talks about 'Vision Boards' and their use in helping to manifest your desired outcomes in his book, *The Success Principles.* On page 117 of that book, you can read about the importance of using visualization in your pursuit of the goals you wish to obtain.

Whether your goal is to build multiple streams of income to provide for yourself and loved ones or to develop a large organization, you will benefit from creating a vision for the future that helps keep you motivated and on track. There will be obstacles and speed bumps along the way that will at times be discouraging and disheartening. That is the time to revisit your vision and reinforce your will and determination that you will reach your goal no matter the circumstances.

You want to keep your vision and goal in writing where you can easily locate it, refer to it when necessary, and measure whether you are staying on track. You should review it at least monthly, preferably once a week. While reviewing it, visualize and feel, with as much emotion as possible, what it will be like when you achieve your objectives. Make it as real as you can in your imagination, so you embed it in your DNA. The more you do this, the easier it becomes to recall it. The more you recall it, the quicker you will achieve it.

Make sure you reward yourself and the people who've helped you when you reach certain goals and objectives, as well as specific milestones on your journey. It will reinforce your efforts and the efforts of those who are helping you.

TIP 9: Set aside time in your day to work on your vision and goals; otherwise, other demands will take over. Schedule reserved time for deep work. You should schedule half the day for deep work and half for shallow work, i.e. meetings, email, phone calls, etc. Also remember,

"What gets scheduled, gets done." Very important! Because it works. Vision without execution is fantasy. If you don't get into action, you'll never achieve what you are visualizing. Perhaps you're struggling with your vision. This is not unusual. It can be a process to identify a vision and takes some soul searching. These quotes will be of some guidance:

"Watch yourself carefully, and you will find running under the wavelets of your many incidental desires an undercurrent of some definite desire. That ignored permanent desire, which has always been with you, coaxing you to listen to it, is the real arch-angel of success you should follow." – Paramahansa Yogananda

"Imagination [the power to image or visualize] is a very important factor in creative thought. But imagination has to be ripened into conviction. You can't do that without a strong will. But if you imagine something with all the power of your will, your imagination will be converted into conviction. And when you can hold that conviction against all odds, it will come true." – Paramahansa Yogananda

Many of the books on goal setting and peak performance discuss visualization as a critical component. Being able to visualize the end result, goal, or objective, as well as the actual image and experience in your mind's eye, will help you to manifest it.

High performance athletes have been practicing visualization for decades and have broken world records. People in various professions have been using it with equally impressive results.

When you replay the performance or required skillset in your mind over and over, in detail, it programs your mind and nervous system to act according to your practice when it is performed in real life. You end up manifesting your dreams and objectives the way you experienced them when practicing your visualizations.

It takes perseverance, dedication, and relentless action to bring it all together, but your visualization is what provides the matrix for the pieces to come together. It is metaphysical in the respect that what you visualize, believe, and act upon will come about just as it does in the dream world, only this is the physical world we're discussing.

Visualization is a two-edged sword. If you dwell on and visualize negative scenarios with strong feelings and emotions, you can bring about those things in your life. That's why it's critically important to monitor your thoughts and keep them positive.

Our universe is made up of energy. This has been proven scientifically almost 100 years ago with the invention of the electro-magnetic microscope. When scientists could examine atoms close up, they found that they were swirling with protons and neutrons. Einstein said that we exist in and are a mass of swirling energy.

Japanese author, Masaru Emoto did a study of drops of water under a high-powered microscope. In his book, "The Hidden Messages of Water," he describes how he conducted his experiments. He played classical music while observing and photographing water molecules. He found them to be beautifully shaped cells not unlike snowflakes, each with their own unique designs and patterns. When he played loud heavy metal rock music, they took on deformed, ugly looking patterns and designs. The same happened when he spoke lovingly to them and when he screamed and yelled in a denigrating manner. The droplets of water are composed of energy and reacting to the energy surrounding it. It is a very interesting study that really underscores the fact that everything is energy.

This is a subject that most of us give little thought to, but the underlying effects are far reaching when you consider that our thoughts are energy. What we think has a direct effect on our physical beings, our environment and all that we come into contact with. Don't believe it? Ever been somewhere when someone who's depressed or angry, fearful, uptight or upset enters the room? They don't have to speak a word. You can tell by the vibrations they are putting out that their thoughts are causing a different feeling in the room than existed before they entered.

> **TIP 10:** Our thoughts are very powerful, and we need to be keenly aware of what we allow to enter our consciousness. That energy has a direct effect on our being and our world. Not paying attention to it is just allowing things to roll out according to happenstance, which, depending upon our everyday mental habits and thoughts, will either bring us success or failure, whichever is strongest.

ACTION ITEMS

✔ Take time to focus on and explore what your vision is.

✔ Develop a visualization exercise that you can practice daily for your vision of what your goals and objectives are. Doing this first thing in the morning is best because your mind is fresh and open to new thoughts. You can also do it when you are in bed getting ready to fall asleep, when you're slipping into the subconscious. Find a quiet place where you can sit and close your eyes while you go through the exercise. The more often you do it, the easier it will be to recall. If you do it at various times of the day, your results will manifest sooner.

✔ Write out your visualization in detail, with all of the feelings and emotions you would feel when you have obtained or accomplished it. Place it on your smartphone or a note card and commit it to memory.

✔ Get the book or audiobook *Vivid Vision*, by Cameron Herold. It's an excellent start to putting your vision in place and walking you through the process.

Chapter 5

ATTITUDE OF GRATITUDE: SUPERCHARGE YOUR DAILY LIFE

There's always something that we can be grateful for. I say this because we all take so many blessings in our lives for granted. The benefit of practicing gratitude is that it not only makes you focus on the positive things you have in your life, which makes you feel grateful, but it also opens a channel for more positive things to come to you. That's a universal law that is irrefutable. It works even more effectively if you add in the Law of Positive Expectation.

> *"When you are grateful, fear disappears, and abundance appears."*
> – Tony Robbins

We often view certain occurrences in our lives as bad luck. However, as time goes on, we see that many times, those occurrences were actually blessings. The longer you live, the more you see that.

I would say that my daily practice of gratitude has made a huge difference in my life. I start each day with appreciation for all the things I have in my life that God has given me. That doesn't mean that everything goes smoothly, all the time. It doesn't. All I need to do when things seem to be moving in a tough direction is to remind myself of all the good things I have to be grateful for.

A simple way to start this habit is to create a gratitude journal. First thing in the morning, when you're having a cup of coffee, write down a minimum of three to seven things you have to be grateful for. It doesn't matter how small or insignificant they may seem now. Just put them down on your list. Keep it going for as long as you can. Include things like your pet; your home or apartment; your town or city where you live; your country; the opportunities you've been given; the lessons you've learned; the help you've received. For example: I am happy and grateful for:

My Wife/Husband/Significant Other
My family
My friends
My health
My gifts
My blessings
For all I have

TIP 11: There are gratitude apps you can download onto your smartphone. Carla White offers a wonderful gratitude app that you can download on iTunes and for Android. I've used it for years now and it's great. It is very simple and easy to use, keeps track of your entries, and has extra added features for those who want more from their app. For example, instant access to her 'Radical Shift' podcast, a reminder, and other features. There are plenty of others out there too. Find one that works for you that will help you to develop a gratitude habit.

Once you begin to practice gratitude, you'll be sold on it and want to do it every day because you'll notice how much better you feel when you start your day. You will see that there is much more than you initially thought you had to be grateful for. When I did this exercise, I was happy I had made the effort, because it made me realize I am a very fortunate person. I have much to be grateful for.

We tend to compare our lives to others' because they may have more or seem to be happier and have more fulfilling lives. In reality, most likely that is not the case. There is always much more going on in people's lives than we can see or understand. It's been said that if you knew the thoughts of others, you wouldn't want to change places with them.

Comparing yourself to others is a losing game. There will always be somebody who you think is smarter, richer, happier, handsomer, prettier, etc.

Be happy with what you have and where you are. Learn to be content and even-minded, no matter what is going on in your life. That doesn't mean you shouldn't strive to improve your life and surroundings if that's what you want. But don't think that that is what's going to make you happy. Happiness is an inside job. You need to make up your mind to be happy wherever you are and in whatever you're doing. Then you can be happy anywhere at any time.

When you practice cultivating an attitude of gratitude, life is richer, happier, and easier.

ACTION ITEMS

✔ Make your list of all the things you have to be grateful for. Keep it handy so that you can look at it occasionally to remind yourself that you have much to be thankful for. And be sure to thank God for all you have every day. He's the Giver of ALL gifts.

✔ Start a daily gratitude journal or download a gratitude app on your smartphone that you can write in each morning before getting your day started.

Chapter 6

DEVELOP NEW HABITS

We can make our lives easier with good habits or become slaves to our bad habits. We can be our own best friend or our own worst enemy, based upon the habits we condition ourselves by. The bad habits we have created can be insidious and constantly working against us. We may not even be aware of them. That's why it's critical to be introspective and look for those habits of thought to see which ones are working for and against us.

> *"It isn't what you have, or who you are, or where you are, or what you are doing that makes you happy or unhappy. It is what you think about."*
>
> – Dale Carnegie

They show up in our conversations, our responses, our interactions with others and in all manner of ways throughout our lives. Many have been ingrained by our upbringing, whether by our parents and home environment, our community, our culture, or a combination of them all.

Knowing this is half the battle. Instead of blaming circumstances or others, we must take responsibility for our own thinking and self-improvement, knowing we are in the end, the only ones who are in control of our thinking. Only then we can begin to mold our own consciousness and thought patterns in a positive direction.

First, we must decide that we will start to make a conscious effort daily to transform our thinking process with only positive thoughts. That doesn't mean we will always be able to maintain that method of thinking. Negative events and life problems and issues will continue to enter our lives. What's important is that you immediately point your thoughts in a positive direction when you realize you're thinking negatively. Remember, you are establishing a new habit that requires repetition.

TIP 12: The old school of thought was that it takes 21 days to establish a new habit. New psychological studies have shown that it takes much longer. Think of your brain as an old-time phonograph player. When the record player's needle was placed on the record it would play that song. Your brain works similarly, in that the neural pathways in your brain are like the grooves in a record. It takes time to install a new habit in your neural pathways (brain grooves). Each time you perform the habit, that groove becomes deeper and more established, making it easier for the repetitive task or thought to be installed and played back.

The key to getting rid of a bad habit is to replace it with a good habit. For example, if you love to eat junk food snacks such as potato chips or cookies, you should prep some healthier snacks such as chopped vegetables or fruits and place them in small sandwich bags in the refrigerator. Then, when you go to the kitchen for a snack, grab a small bag of your healthy snack instead of the potato chips, cookies, candies, or whatever your not-so-healthy snack choice was. The important thing is to reinforce the new habit each time by getting back on track as soon as possible if you fall back. Don't get discouraged. Keep trying until your new habit is iron-clad and automatic.

An excellent way to reinforce your new habit is to think of a reward for yourself when you reach certain milestones, such as one week, one month, or whatever goal you set. Make sure the reward is one that motivates you. It doesn't have to be crazy or exorbitant. Save those for hitting the bigger milestones and goals.

It is recommended that you don't try to change more than three habits at a time before they're established. Otherwise, you become overwhelmed and discouraged. Then, you'll want to throw in the towel and say forget it.

Establishing new good habits creates a momentum that makes you want to continue replacing old negative habits with new positive ones.

Exercising is a habit we all should cultivate. People who have an aversion to it need to start out with small incremental positive changes. For example, create a daily regimen of walking around the block or up the street and back the first week. Then go two blocks the next, gradually increasing the distance each week, but making sure you do your daily walk. This builds the habit more quickly and motivates you to continue. Especially when you begin to experience the benefits of exercising.

Don't go to the gym five days in a row and injure yourself or get so sore it takes a week or more to feel normal again. That's a sure recipe for demotivating you away from exercising. Start off gradually, with small incremental increases to build upon. Give yourself the 30-day trial of two to three days a week to see how you're feeling. Then, give it another 30-day trial after that. You'll feel much better and want to continue.

In a research study, bio-scientists found that those who ate a healthy diet while starting an exercise routine experienced greater results than those who continued to eat a carbohydrate rich diet with little to no fresh vegetables and fruits. The bottom line is diet is 50% of the health enhancing program when it comes to exercising. To continue to eat fatty foods and diet drinks (which has been found to increase weight) and expect big benefits from your new exercise program is unrealistic. If you're going to exercise and start your new health regimen, why not eat properly as well? Then you can be assured that the benefits will be forthcoming in just a matter of time.

TIP 13: Another way to install a new habit is to mark off a day on a calendar, and keep it where you can see it daily. Put a big X on the day each time you perform your new routine. In time, it will reinforce your efforts and you'll want to see a full month crossed off each day representing your objective.

TIP 14: Affirmations are another way to program your thinking. If constructed and carried out properly, your affirmations can catapult your efforts. The important thing about affirmations is that they must be stated in the first person (I) and as though you are experiencing the benefit you are stating in the present tense. For example, "I feel more energy now that I'm exercising daily and eating healthy foods. Each day my energy level is increasing, and I feel healthier than ever."

It is important not to create too long a list of affirmations. Start out with no more than five or six. Close your eyes and visualize yourself accomplishing those objectives, feeling the benefits and experiencing all that you would as if you already had those traits, achievements, and benefits, that you're looking to obtain. The more emotion you add, the faster the results. Don't forget, you must also be doing the things necessary to accomplish them. They will come about in due time.

When trying to break a bad habit, try "won't" power instead of will power. Just say, "I won't do it," and divert your attention to something else more constructive, e.g. reading or listening to motivational information, or even taking a walk.

"It is not your passing inspirations or brilliant ideas so much as your everyday mental habits that control your life. Habits of thought are mental magnets that draw to you certain things, people, and conditions. Good habits of thought enable you to attract benefits and opportunities. Bad habits of thought attract you to materially minded persons and to unfavorable environments."- Paramahansa Yogananda

Replacing old bad habits with new good ones is not always easy, but the rewards far outweigh the effort expended. Remember, it's just repetition of the habit you are seeking to install. Keep at it and don't give up until it becomes part of you.

ACTION ITEMS

- ✔ Take inventory and make a list of the bad habits you'd like to remove from your life.

- ✔ Decide and prioritize the top three habits you wish to replace first.

- ✔ Make a list of the new habits you want to install, including which bad habits will be replaced by the new ones if applicable.

- ✔ Create a list of affirmations for the things you want to change for yourself. Then, start using them on a daily basis.

- ✔ Create a plan to start the process, and decide on the rewards you will give yourself once you hit your set milestones.

Chapter 7

THE ANCIENT GREEKS KNEW: STRONG BODY, STRONG MIND

We've all heard the old axiom *"Strong body, strong mind."* What the ancient Greeks were essentially teaching us was that it's easier to proceed in life when you're feeling healthy and vibrant with energy, than when you're not. They were big believers in regular physical conditioning combined with the benefits of mental training.

It's hard to feel motivated and up-beat if your energy levels are low and you're feeling out-of-shape and weak.

A major priority should be to have some type of physical regimen to stay fit; even as simple as going for a walk

"Fatigue doth make cowards of us all."
– Green Bay Packers coach Vince Lombardi

outdoors each day for fresh air as well as to get the circulation moving. Do a minimum of 30 minutes of exercise daily.

It's easy to be lazy and not try to make an effort to stay in shape. Especially if the weather is bad or you haven't done it in a while. The benefits are too great not to be doing it. As health professionals like to tell us, "If you're too busy to exercise today, you are too busy." The crazy thing is that once you make it a habit you don't want to *not do it* because you feel much better when you do.

You'll feel more energetic, positive, happy, and motivated and less stressed. You also sleep better, look better, and think more clearly.

The other requirement for having a strong mind and strong body is to eat the right foods to provide you with the energy needed to exercise and perform at your best.

Most people put more thought into planning their vacations than planning their meals and eating right. If you only started there, you would see a major improvement in your energy levels and the way you feel. It is that critical. You wouldn't give a thoroughbred horse junk food and expect them to perform at their peak. It works the same with your body's chemistry.

TIP 15: A major game-changer health wise for me was when I read the book *Eat to Live*, by Dr. Joel Fuhrman, a former Olympic athlete and world-renowned physician. His book is a bestseller on Amazon and has changed the lives of hundreds of thousands of people. He uses the latest scientific findings to back up his research. His proof is through his medical practice with the many people he has saved from the brink of death by helping them turn their lives around with his diet advice. I was eating what I thought was a healthy diet until I read that book and was introduced to new scientific findings I hadn't been aware of.

Dr. Fuhrman shows you that you don't have to deny yourself your favorite foods, like pizza, ice cream, greasy hamburgers, french fries, etc., as long as you're not eating them as part of your regular diet regimen. He suggests giving his philosophy a try and seeing how you feel.

I thought, sure. Why not? I gave myself 30 days to see if I noticed a difference. What I found was I had more energy; my sinus issues cleared up, and I was breathing better than I had in years; I was sleeping more soundly and felt more restful when

I got up in the morning. The other benefit I saw, which surprised me, was that I lost 12 pounds without even trying. I was not even hungry while I was following his advice. I was sold on his suggested changes and began to permanently alter my diet routine. I still follow it today with the same terrific results.

Ultimately, Dr. Fuhrman showed me that diet is just a habit. Once you establish the habit, you don't even have to think about. It just comes automatically and naturally.

If you implement these suggestions and recommendations into your life, you will see a major positive difference, and you will be glad you took action.

TIP 16: Another suggestion I have for you is to try implementing a yoga routine into your lifestyle. It has many health benefits and is a great way to de-stress your body and mind. Even a couple of times each week has noticeable benefits that you'll want to continue once experienced.

I started yoga about six years ago when a friend of mine suggested I look into it. I had been experiencing chronic back pain for some time. I'd get over it for a short while and then I'd do something at the gym to trigger more back pain. I was constantly taking one step forward and two steps backwards with my back issues.

My friend told me he was having similar issues with his back and decided to give yoga a try. Once he started making it part of his weekly routine, he said his back problems disappeared. That's all I needed to hear to push me into trying it. I never looked back after I did. I started out with taking a class twice a week after work. I started feeling more relaxed and my lower back was getting stronger. My sciatica pain was disappearing and no longer a regular issue from all the sitting I was doing during the day. I was becoming more flexible and felt that my muscles were less tight when I first got up in the morning. I'll stick with yoga for as long as I'm able to. It's something you can do well into your old age.

Yoga is easy on the joints and anyone can practice it on some level. There are even gentle chair yoga classes on YouTube for those who need them. It helps keep you flexible, improves circulation, stimulates the nervous system, strengthens your immune system, and aids your digestion system, among many other benefits.

One of the hardest yoga classes I've ever experienced was led by an 84-year-old teacher. She said, if you want to be able to move like me when you get to be my age, keep practicing yoga. That sold me. There are way too many benefits to derive from yoga to not do it.

ACTION ITEMS

✔ If you don't already have a fitness program or regimen you follow, decide to implement one today. 'Just do it', like the Nike advertisements say. You will notice the difference, and success begets success.

✔ If you haven't read the book, *Eat to Live*, by Dr. Joel Fuhrman, order it today. It's even available as an audiobook on Audible.com. I promise that you will learn a lot about nutrition, and you'll be motivated to try his recommendations out. If you order the book, don't be intimidated; half of it is delicious recipes. I promise you won't be disappointed.

✔ Check out a yoga studio online or in your area. At the back of this book I have the contact information for my yoga teacher. Mahnaz has been teaching for 20 years. I've been to many different yoga classes, and she's the best teacher I've found. She has students of all types and ages, as well as celebrities and world class athletes. She makes it enjoyable. She has classes online. Her website is www.samadiyoga.com.

Chapter 8

CLEAN UP YOUR MESSES

If there's anything new that you want to show up in your life, you've got to make room for it.

Cleaning up your messes may sound simplistic, and it is, but it's a powerful concept that, if understood and implemented the right way, can play a significant role in achieving success.

I've seen it work in my own life. The principle works like this: Make a list of all of the messes in your life, home, office, personal finances, and any other areas you feel need cleaning up. For example, your closets, the garage, attic, drawers, office, file cabinets, etc. This can also entail mending relationships that have been abandoned or left with issues unresolved, forgiving others, apologizing, or any other unsettled matters. Perhaps you've been thinking about creating a will, a living trust or health directives for yourself and your spouse but haven't gotten around to it. Or you're still deciding on that life insurance policy you researched years ago.

> *"Small steps make big changes."*
> - Jack Canfield,
> *The Success Principles*

Organize your clean-up list by creating categories like home, office, personal, or relationships. Once you have made a clean-up list in each category, place a completion date next to each goal. It's important to be realistic and not overly ambitious. Then, make it a goal to work on at least one daily. Some you may be able to complete in one day; others will take longer. Don't worry about that, as long as you're making progress.

The result is that you will feel a level of accomplishment with each task tackled and completed. Each finished item will build upon the others, creating a powerful momentum. It's a terrific feeling to experience when you see your life becoming more orderly in all departments. You'll see the benefits spill over into other areas in your life just by clearing out the clutter, making way for more positive energy to manifest those things you're looking to make happen.

TIP 17: One of the more important time management and clean up tricks I learned in Jack Canfield's book, *The Success Principles*, is "The 4 Ds of Completion." It's essentially a clever organizational system to take care of to-do items. You may be familiar with the concept. The 4 Ds are: Do it, Delegate it, Delay it, or Dump it. If you pick up a document or paper, decide then and there what your choice is. If you can't handle it in less than five minutes, dump it. If you can, do it right away. If you still want to do it, but it's going to take longer, create a file to place those items in.

If you can't do it yourself or don't have time, delegate it to someone else that you feel will handle it properly. Have them let you know when they've completed the task.

It's important that once you've completed your list of things to clean up and checked them off, you continue to stay on top of those items that tend to clutter your environment. I'm sure you know what I'm referring to. The stack of books you have on your nightstand next to your bed you're going to read someday. The stack of magazines or periodicals you don't want to throw out because you haven't gotten around to reading through them yet. If you don't manage this clutter, it can get out of hand quickly, which starts the whole insidious habit cycle again.

TIP 18: In *The Success Principles* on page 250, Jack Canfield shares a list of 25 ideas to start cleaning up your life. By the way, the book, which is a classic in the self-help category, is one of the best I've come across. My copy has been read through several times and is highlighted, underscored and written in the margins, over and over. It's one those books that should be reviewed on an annual basis.

As I like to recite regularly, *"We need reminding as much as we need learning."*

ACTION ITEMS

✔ Sit down and create your list of items and messes you want to clean up in your life. Take time to think through it. It's worth the effort. Choose one item and get started. Keep working on your list each day. Before long you'll have it completed and feel fantastic about the results.

✔ Order a copy of *The Success Principles*. Read a chapter each day. This will turbo-charge your efforts and your game plan for your life. It will also keep you motivated.

✔ Get the book or audiobook, *The Life Changing Magic of Tidying Up* by Marie Kondo.

Chapter 9

SIMPLIFY

We have a tendency as humans to complicate our lives by adding more wants and activities. Part of it is seeing others acquiring the latest cars, TVs, smartphones, and clothing, going on exotic vacations, and the list goes on.

What we need is to learn to separate our wants from our needs. Our wants are endless; our needs are few.

There are multiple benefits of simplifying our lives. The less we have to deal with, the less cluttered our minds

"Control your life; make it as simple as you can. Have money in the bank for emergencies. Save more than you spend on unnecessary necessities. And always include someone else in your happiness."

– Paramahansa Yogananda

become and the more clearly we can think. We can slow down and enjoy our everyday pleasures. We can focus more on our families, friends, relationships, hobbies, and ourselves.

Many people are fitting way too many activities into their lives in order to feel fulfilled, make sure their kids are fully occupied, or keep themselves busy. The problem is that when there's no downtime, there's no decompression that can take place. It's like being on a hamster wheel, with no end in sight, until something or someone breaks. You can liken it to putting 2000 volts through a 50-watt light bulb. You're placing too much strain on your nervous system. Eventually it burns out.

It's super important that we build downtime into our day. That may come first thing in the morning, before we get our day started and when everyone else is still asleep. It may require you to get up an hour earlier, but once the habit is established you will relish it. It's your uninterrupted alone time, your golden hour. You can read, meditate, pray, study, or whatever you decide would be something you'd find helpful or enjoyable.

TIP 19: Hal Elrod, author of the #1 international bestseller, *The Miracle Morning*, says that simplifying your life and having a morning routine to start your day can change your entire life. Do yourself a favor and check it out. You'll see why so many others have rated his books and podcast so highly. This powerful routine has an incredible impact and payback from the time spent to set the tone for your day.

Start asking questions when coming across the things and situations you'd like to simplify: *Do I need this? Do I have to do this? Is this necessary? Is this worth my time? What's more important? Where is my time best spent? What do I really want to spend my time doing with this?* Questions are the starting point for change. By learning how to use questions to simplify your everyday world, you can bring clarity to a confusing and complicated situation.

TIP 20: Think of ways to automate and optimize your work and personal life. That can include hiring a virtual assistant to handle certain tasks where your time can be put to better use to create more value. Again, there are plenty of resources, such as upwork.com, freelancer.

com, etc., that you can tap into. You can automate bill-pay for your bills online. You can hire others to run errands, walk your dog, pick up your dry cleaning, fix things around the house, etc.

Think of things you can cut down or cut out of your life, such as TV, internet, and social media time, because it is easy to get sucked into their time vortex. Cut out social events that you feel an obligation to attend but don't necessarily enjoy. Many times you go mainly out of habit or because your friend wants you there with them. We all have some type of similar habitual time wasters that we've gone on autopilot with for years.

Stop multi-tasking and replace with single-tasking, doing as many things in your day as possible with a single-pointed mind. Put 100% focus on that task and give your full attention toward whatever you're doing. Make it a point to focus on one thing at a time instead of bouncing around, especially at work, the easiest place to fall into the trap of multi-tasking.

By scheduling your day, you'll be allowing yourself to concentrate and focus on those tasks which require no distractions and deeper thinking. Consistently being distracted and interrupted makes it difficult to accomplish those tasks necessary to create progress. You will see a dramatic difference in your work quality when you adopt this practice.

TIP 21: As you have probably figured out, I like to use tools to help me reach my goals. One smartphone app I am particularly a fan of is based on the Pomodoro Method. The app is called *Be Focused Pro*. Many similar apps are available, but this one works well for me. It's basically a timer with reminders. It features work intervals that can be set for various times, with short and long breaks after a series of work intervals. These can be time adjusted as you desire. Mine is set as follows:

- Work Interval: 40 minutes
- Short Interval: 10 minutes (Break)
- Long Break: 15 minutes

- Long Break After: 4 Intervals
- Target: 8-10 Intervals per Day

Creating a system, like this timer, keeps you focused and disciplined and allows you to stay on track. I've found it to be a big help when working on projects, such as writing this book.

Another way to simplify your life is to give away any need-less possessions. It's as easy as it sounds. Believe it or not, you'll feel terrific when you've finished going through your closets, drawers, rooms, and garage and donated things you no longer need or use. Heck, you can even have a garage sale, if you're up for it. Then, do something fun with the money or donate it to one of your favorite causes.

Start looking into the things you buy and consume, so you can determine what is necessary for you to own. Consider if what you're buying is something you really need or want or if something or a combination of things you already own can take care of the same purpose. Going through the thought process will force you to determine if it's something you can do without. I find that many times I talk myself out of things because I realize they are not an absolute necessity for me to have. It may be nice to own, but I've found many things are just that. Something that would be nice to have. Then, I have to figure out how to get rid of it someday.

ACTION ITEMS

- ✔ Come up with a list of things you can do to start simplifying your life.
- ✔ What tasks and jobs can you delegate, automate, or optimize?
- ✔ What can you eliminate from your life that creates stress and anxiety that you can do without? Who can you hire or outsource to for proper handling?

Chapter 10

YOUR ENVIRONMENTS: INSPIRING OR EXPIRING YOU?

Your environments have an inordinate impact on your daily life, your mental outlook, and everything you do.

Everything is environment. Everything is energy. Everything is connected. Your energy is directly affected by the environment you are in and surrounded by. Even your calendar is an environment. Environment affects your mindset, moods, thinking processes, and myriad other factors that create the world around you.

It is critically important that we are keenly aware of our environments and how they can help or hinder that which we are trying to be, do, or become.

Environment is stronger than will power!

It's been said that if you want to become an artist, then you should hang out with artists. If you want to become a proficient musician, you should spend

> "The greatest influence in your life, stronger even than your will power, is your environment. Change that if necessary."
> – Paramahansa Yogananda

time with musicians. If you want to become a successful businessperson, spend time around people who are successful in the business you're interested in.

When I first got into the commercial real estate business, I was fortunate to be surrounded by several successful commercial agents. I was a sponge for new information and was constantly asking what I could do to help them. Eventually I earned their respect and they would offer me suggestions and help. They also invited me to work on projects with them. I made sure I was always going the extra mile in whatever I was asked to do to. Eventually, I was doing the things they were doing and getting similar results.

The point is that when you're in an environment where others are high performing individuals in their craft, you're going to be heavily influenced by their words and actions. This pertains to all lines of work and endeavors.

Design your environments so that they support your goals and objectives. Your environments are working on you 24/7.

I'll give you a brief overview of how environments work on our psyche and worlds. They have a direct effect on our beliefs, which directly impact our actions, emotions and behaviors.

There are ten primary environments that directly affect our individual world. They are:

1. You– The core of you that is unchanging
2. Memetic Beliefs– Ideas, knowledge, cultural norms, frameworks
3. Body– Physical body, health, energy
4. Self– Personality, gifts, talents, strengths, emotions
5. Spirit– Connection to a higher source, love
6. Relationships– Family, friends, close colleagues, support personnel
7. Network– Community, strategic partners, customers
8. Finance– Money, investments, budgeting, insurance
9. Surroundings– Home, furnishings, equipment/technology
10. Nature– Outdoors, beauty, seasons, cycle of life

Each environment is impacted by the other. If we are weaker in one area it will have a direct effect on the others.

TIP 22: I first learned of the environment concept through a coaching program I went through with Jack Canfield and Patty Aubery called, "Success Principles Coaching Club." Jim Bunch, a peak performance coach at The Ultimate Game of Life, was a guest speaker. As he addressed this concept, it resonated with me in such a way that I immediately wanted to start implementing the ideas he put forth in many areas of my life. You can download his self-assessment exercise and explanation called "9 Environments Assessments" PDF at www.unmistakablecreative.com. It's very powerful and will underscore and highlight where you may need improvement in your own environments. Also, check out Jack Canfield's Blog at JackCanfield.com called "Taking Control of the Environments That Control You."

Once you understand the importance of the setting around you and how essential it is to ensure that your environments are supporting you, you will want to always be consciously monitoring them.

Pay attention to environment:
- Start designing and choosing environments so that they support your goals and objectives.
- Clean out your environments.
- Raise your awareness of all of your environments and continuously improve them.
- Orient your life around your values and align yourself with them through your surroundings.

You will benefit from even the small changes you make once you start becoming attuned to each of the nine environments listed earlier. Remember, micro wins every day! As you look for ways to improve them, this process will become automatic.

Here are simple ways to increase awareness of your surroundings and control them. As you're sitting at your desk and you notice that clutter is mounting, stop what you're doing and clear it out. If you're looking to grab a snack or drink, be aware of the choices you make so that they energize you. If you finished dinner and feel like plopping down on the couch, try taking a walk instead and see how that feels. It will step up your metabolism and help your digestive process. Start the process and you'll begin to see the many ways you can make improvements.

Raise the frequency of your environments to align with them. Remember that everything is energy. That means if the energy being created in the environment is not working for your benefit, you are creating a negative frequency or vibration. If there's clutter in your environment, that will create distraction and confusion. You want it to be conducive to your productivity and thinking processes. For example, a clean desk, organized files and papers, work materials in the proper place and easily accessed, etc. This will allow you to focus more clearly and easily.

Choose beliefs that raise your vibration. Your beliefs are the filters you see life through. Your beliefs are your thermometer for the energy vibrations you create in your environments. For example, if you're in a negative state of mind after speaking with someone who is spewing negativity when you speak with them about all the problems in their life, the world and whatever else they're complaining about, that can change your mental energy and affect your environment. That is until you clear your thinking and place your thoughts in a positive direction. Remember, thoughts are energy and have a direct impact on us and our environments.

Never set goals in an environment that you're familiar with. In other words, give yourself a different perspective in another environment that will allow you to be more open and receptive to your new ideas and not distracting or conforming to your everyday mental habits. Maybe take a drive out to the country, mountains, lakeside or beach. Someplace with little or no distractions would be ideal.

Your mindset conforms to whatever environment you're in. If you are trying to brainstorm and set goals (even your goals are an environment) in a surrounding that has distractions or negative memories or people there, it will be more difficult for you. You want to be able to exercise your creative idea muscles and allow your imagination to work freely.

Shift your language patterns and focus on solutions, not problems. Shift your language to emphasize what you want!

Most importantly, surrender to allow the Infinite to work through you! Learn to let go, and let God help and guide you. Give it to God. Don't try to burden yourself with all the troubles and worries that are vexing your thinking. Stay positive and keep working toward your solutions at the same time you are asking for guidance. Know and believe that the right thoughts and results will come in their own time.

ACTION ITEMS

✔ **Download the '9 Environments Assessments' PDF at www.unmistakablecreative.com and go through it.**

✔ **Start developing a plan to improve the environments in your life.**

✔ **Each day, work on making yourself more conscious of your environments and how you can make improvements to them, no matter how small.**

Chapter 11

BE WILLING TO TAKE CRITICISM

Aristotle, in ancient Greek times, was keenly aware that by putting yourself out there, you were potentially subjected to criticism. Some people will even tell you that if you're not a target of criticism, you're probably not trying hard enough.

It's important that you develop a thick skin and not allow negative comments or barbs to affect you. The reality is that some people have to chop off the heads of others to make themselves feel taller. It's generally their own insecurities that are coming out when they feel they have to offer up their two cents worth of opinion.

> *"Learn to accept blame, criticism and accusation silently and without retaliation, even though untrue and unjustified."*
> – Saint Francis of Assisi

I'm not saying it's always easy to hear. The right attitude should be to ask yourself if what they're saying has any merit. If so, then consider what you can do to correct it. If you learn to read and listen to input objectively, without emotion, then you have a better chance of taking it constructively. This does take some practice but is worthwhile.

Remember, when others are trying to get to you and make you angry by their criticisms, they want you to respond angrily. That way they feel they have won their objective. If you don't respond emotionally and you say instead, "Maybe you're right, but I don't think so," they most likely will feel frustrated and leave you alone.

The main thing is to not allow them to drag you into an argument. Just tell them you are happy to discuss whatever they need to, but you're not interested in arguing, because wise people discuss, and fools argue. If they still want to argue, just walk away and let them be. Get away from the situation, if possible, and let them cool off.

Once I learned to take criticism and distance myself from it, I can say that it has defused situations that could have turned out badly. When I come across criticism, I try to remind myself that there may be a lesson in there somewhere. The more you try, the better you get at it. I'm still working at it, but I won't stop until I've mastered it.

I remember back when I was in my late 20s and I was working with a semi-retired gentleman named Burt. We were out to lunch one day, and I was lamenting about something derogatory that someone said about me to another person we worked with. He then told me something that has stuck with me all these years and gave me comfort:

In your 20s, you worry about what others are thinking about you.

In your 30s, you don't care what others are thinking about you.

In your 40s, you realize others weren't even thinking about you. They're too busy thinking about themselves.

It's very true. Most people are thinking about themselves and their own problems and issues and not about yours. So, don't even worry about it. Stay focused on your tasks and objectives.

Tell yourself that you're bulletproof and can take whatever is thrown at you. If you remain calm and even minded under all circumstances, you'll be able to handle anything. If you are in control of your emotions, then you are in control. You'll be able to think clearly and respond calmly.

ACTION ITEMS

✔ **Make up your mind that you will practice distancing yourself emotionally the next time you start to hear someone criticize you. When you feel your emotions begin to rise, say to yourself, "I can remain apart from this feeling," and listen calmly. When they're finished, remain silent for a bit, then speak quietly. You will feel empowered if you maintain your cool.**

✔ **Analyze the criticisms you receive to see if there's any merit to them. If so, develop a plan to correct those faults that were pointed out. This takes patience and willingness to introspect, but it can be a powerful exercise.**

Chapter 12

LEARN TO BE A DEEP LISTENER

We've all been told that listening is an important skill that we should practice and improve. But how many of us do that, and do it well?

This is one skill most all of us could use improvement in. It also has huge potential to help us in many areas in our life. In our personal lives, it will serve to strengthen our connections to those who we love and care about. In our business lives, those who we interact with will feel more connected to us and believe we truly care about them as our customers or clients. In our everyday lives, just about everyone we come into contact with will feel like we're more attentive to them.

Women are generally better than men at it, mainly because they generally are more empathetic. They also tend to communicate better than men. Men have a tendency to want to offer a fix or advice instead of just listening, but most people aren't necessarily looking for solutions. They want to be heard first and foremost.

When people feel they're being listened to empathetically, it builds trust. When you practice being a deep listener you are riveted on the speaker and are listening with all your senses.

You don't interrupt them while they are talking. You acknowledge your understanding and their explanations of their issues, feelings, grievances, or expressions, whatever the case may be. That can be done with a nod of the head, or your eyes may reflect your intent of hearing what they're saying. You may even say something like, "I see what you're saying." Or "I hear what you're saying." Or even, "I understand why you're feeling that way."

The important thing is to be sincere. If you aren't, the other person will pick up on that and will disregard any empathy you were trying to convey.

We have all felt what it's like when you're being listened to intently and empathetically. It can be a cathartic experience when you have someone to express your feelings and frustrations to. Even if they simply sit and listen to you in a deep manner and offer no advice. We go away feeling like we had a load lifted off of our shoulders.

TIP 23: The more emotionally charged the speaker is, the more important it is to remain calm and listen. This takes practice, but you will see that the other person will calm down after they've had a chance to vent their frustrations. That doesn't mean you have to sit there and agree with them or take any verbal abuse. You shouldn't be a doormat for anybody.

The important thing to remember is to pause before speaking to them in a calm voice. Then say, "I've heard what you said. Let me restate what I believe you just told me so I'm clear on what you said." By doing this they will feel like you were truly listening to them, instead of thinking about what you're going to say when they are finished. Secondly, many times you will hear that what you thought they said was different from what they were trying to communicate.

TIP 24: If you're meeting someone or a group in a business setting, then take notes while others are speaking. This practice has numerous benefits. First, it forces you to listen carefully while making notes. The other person or people will feel like you're listening intently to them. It also gives you a chance to collect your thoughts for a response to them.

Remember, listening builds trust. When people believe you're giving them your undivided attention and are truly interested in hearing what you have to say, you will have built a communication bridge that will allow for a stronger understanding and connection with them. If you want to be more in tune with those you are looking to do business with, no matter what your endeavor or line of work is, then you want to become proficient at being a good listener and exercising deep listening.

ACTION ITEMS

✔ Start practicing becoming a deep listener when speaking with others. It takes practice, and lots of it.

✔ Practice pausing two to three seconds before responding. Make sure that they've completed the expression of their thoughts before you respond.

✔ It is super-important to listen to your spouse or significant other. I highly recommend the worldwide bestselling book or audiobook, **The Five Love Languages,** by **Gary Chapman**. It is a major game-changer for people striving to be better communicators with their spouses or partners.

Chapter 13

STAY FOCUSED ON YOUR CORE VALUES

One of the more important things we need to remind ourselves while working on achieving our goals and objectives is to keep our core values top of mind. If we fail to do that, we run the risk of getting caught up in the busy work of it all, or the wrong goal, and lose sight of what is important to our main values and objectives.

You may have heard the saying, "Pay attention to the ladder of success you're climbing. You may find it's leaning against the wrong building." Meaning, if it's just money you're trying to amass, you'll find that you may get there, but the personal cost will have been too high. That can mean losing relationships, time to spend with loved ones, your health, or your peace of mind.

When I was 25, I was driving across the country during a summer road trip. I was in the middle of nowhere, driving through Colorado when I was searching for a radio station to listen to. All I was getting was static and jumbled radio signals. I turned it off for a while, then I tried again after about an hour. When I turned it back on again, I eventually hit a talk radio station that was a host interviewing someone. I figured it was better than nothing because it was coming in mostly clear, and I needed some type of entertainment.

As it turned out, the person being interviewed was W. Clement Stone, who was a business icon and one of the richest men in the world at the time. He was also the editor of "Success" magazine which I subscribed to. It was one of the most interesting interviews I had ever heard.

The interviewer asked some in-depth questions and started getting into his personal life. He asked him if he had to do anything over again, after achieving all that he had, what would he have done differently?

What he said stuck with me all these years. He said he had many blessings in his life, but his one big regret was that he spent too much time on his business and not enough time on his family life and his relationships. It cost him dearly, and the cost was irreversible.

TIP 25: When it comes to your hierarchy of values, you should be clear as to what you stand for and what you will not tolerate. For example, if peace of mind is at the top of your list of values, you won't let anything interfere with that. Even if it means passing on a client who is difficult to deal with or a transaction that you believe involves unethical individuals because you know it will affect your peace of mind. Being clear on your hierarchy of values list makes your decision-making process easier and clear cut. It also has the added benefit of steering you away from those circumstances that will end up costing you more than it's worth.

We all have horror stories from our past when we ignored our better judgement and decided to go ahead anyway, only to wish we would have heeded our instincts. When your gut or heart tells you, "this doesn't feel right," or there are indicators and red flags that are popping up, don't ignore them. We sometimes tend to ignore or downplay these signs in order to justify our decisions. You know exactly what I mean. It's called information bias. For example, "They're much too nice. They would never try to do anything like that," or, "That isn't like them. They've been so helpful and cooperative. It's too out of character."

I can think of many times when I've ignored telltale signs from people who I just didn't want to believe were capable of doing anything wrong or improper, or those signs that were subtle but were indicators of flashing yellow lights ahead.

We can't be right 100% of the time, but we can do our best to limit ourselves from making those kinds of misjudgments. Our intuition becomes stronger the more we heed its signs. The calmer you are, the easier it is to recognize those intuitive warnings.

Women seem to have a better intuitive sense because they're more in touch with their emotions and feelings than men. Men can certainly heighten their intuitive sense simply by paying more attention to it. The more tuned in we are to our intuition, the sharper it becomes and the better we get at paying attention to it.

Coming up with your hierarchy list of values may take some introspection and time. Usually, you can easily come up with three to six because you are automatically attentive to them. For example:

- Peace of mind
- Faith
- Family
- Health
- Finances
- Physical fitness

You need to decide your hierarchy of values and prioritize them, so you are clear on exactly what they are. You should also know how your priorities will work when you must make decisions that affect you and them.

ACTION ITEMS

✔ Spend time thinking about your personal hierarchy of values.

✔ Once you have your list, prioritize it according to importance to you.

✔ Remind yourself periodically of this list until you have it memorized and embedded in your psyche.

✔ Live by these values. When you ignore them, you will feel out of sync. Your whole being will let you know.

Chapter 14

STAY FLEXIBLE

L ife has a way of forcing change on us when we aren't open to being flexible. Since it is inevitable that changes are always going to be part of the program of life, why not go with the flow and accept it as one of life's many lessons? That doesn't mean it's always going to be easy, but it's easier when we learn to accept it and adjust our attitude towards it.

We have a tendency as humans to sometimes fall back into our old habits of thinking and re-acting. Some of these habits are deeply ingrained into our sub-conscious minds. It takes effort to change these thought patterns and habits. You may start listening to your mind chatter about how "things don't work out for you" while you're trying to learn new skills, about how "you're not cut out for" whatever you're trying to adjust to in your life or new changes, etc.

> *"Follow your bliss and don't be afraid, and doors will open where you didn't know they were going to be."*
> -Joseph Campbell

If you are working at learning new skills or trying to change occupations, you must remember that everything is difficult before it is easy. Everyone starts out from the same place when learning new skills. Give yourself time and patience. Know that you're capable of learning new things.

Many times, your reaction is "Why is this happening?" or "I can't believe this is what I have to deal with now." Your blood pressure rises, your heart is pounding, and you feel the anxiety welling up within you as you foresee all the difficulties you now have to face.

Yes, this is an occurrence that happens more than we like to think about. However, it's the pause, the second thought you choose for how you are going to deal with it, that makes the difference. First, we should decide to stay calm and re-laxed about our response so that we can come up some viable alternatives.

I can hear it now, "Easy for you to say, because you're not dealing with my issues." That's true, but you do have a choice as to how you react to changes that come your way. If you make up your mind that you are the one in control of your thoughts and emotions, you can choose to be calm about it.

TIP 26: Here is a tip worth remembering. Next time you are in a situation or circumstance which requires you to assess your response to it, remember this and how it works so you may be able to reframe your negative response: Jack Canfield teaches a formula in, *The Success Principles Workbook*, E+R=O, that is, Event + Response = Outcome. There are only three responses you have control over: *behavior, thoughts, and images*. The more you work at controlling these responses, the better you'll become at it, until it becomes automatic. When you control your response to an event, you control the outcome.

You may be familiar with the saying, *"What you resist will persist."* If you don't learn to handle your responses, they will continue to present themselves until you do. Learn the lesson, so you can move on. Otherwise, you'll have to learn it sometime in the future.

TIP 27: Here's an excellent technique to release stress you can try next time you feel tension and are overwhelmed by your daily work and life loads:

- Find a quiet spot where you can sit in a chair (armless if possible).
- Sit up straight with your eyes closed and your hands resting on your lap at the center of your abdomen.
- Inhale deeply to the count of six, filling your lungs. Then tense all the muscles of your body simultaneously to the count of six.
- Slowly exhale to the count of six while relaxing all your muscles, visualizing the tension escaping through your outgoing breath.
- Repeat for a total of three times.
- After the third time, inhale and exhale your breath twice, then let the breath come in and out naturally.
- Once you start breathing naturally, relax and observe your breath go in and out as if you're another person observing your breathing. Enjoy the relaxed feeling for as long as you like but try to stay seated for at least five minutes.
- If you desire, while you're still seated and relaxed with your eyes closed, go back to a time in your mind when you felt totally at peace, enjoying the calmness and serenity of the location that you were in when you experienced it. Try to mentally place yourself back there reliving it like a mini vacation. Maybe it's a beach where you were lying down on the sand with the warm sun on your face and the ocean breeze caressing you as you felt your body weighed down on your towel or blanket. Perhaps you were walking in the woods where the sun was streaming through the trees, and you could hear the birds singing and the wind rustling through the leaves. Choose your own favorite quiet and relaxing spot that you have in your memory.

You'll find this technique to be a great way to release tension and calm your mind and body. You'll be surprised how well this can work when you practice it. It can work wonders if you're having a stressful day and are in need of a mental break.

When you have the mental tools and techniques available to you to deal with the inevitable changes and stress that happen in life, you're better able to stay flexible and handle just about anything that's thrown at you. The first thing is to decide that you're going to start living that way and develop your strategies for handling it.

I'll talk more about one of the best ways I know how to cope with everyday stress and tensions in the next chapter.

ACTION ITEMS

✔ Decide to start working on handling the stress and tension you feel in life when curve balls are thrown at you and develop strategies like the technique mentioned in this chapter.

✔ Try incorporating meditation into your daily routine, so you can create the center of calm in your mind to visit when the storms of life kick up.

✔ Find guided meditations to talk you through the process while you're meditating. There are wonderful options at www.yogananda-srf.org. They are a great introduction to meditation and the benefits derived.

Chapter 15

MEDITATION:
IT'S NOT WHAT YOU THINK

The title of this chapter is a saying I saw on a t-shirt some-one was wearing. It's even more apt if you're familiar with meditation. The practice of meditation is to eliminate extraneous thoughts and fo-cus on an aspect of God, such as peace, joy, love, or some other concept of the Infinite. At the same time, you're calming your breath, slowing your heartbeat, and releasing tensions from your body, so your entire being is calm and centered.

Once you have learned to do this, which happens with some practice, it is easier to reach the calm, centered state where you can experience the peace and joy that comes with the absence of motion, tension,

> *"Uniting the soul with Spirit is Yoga — reunion with that great Happiness everyone is seeking. Isn't this a wonderful definition? In the ever-new Bliss of Spirit you are convinced that the joy you feel is greater than any other happiness, and nothing can get you down."*
>
> -Paramahansa Yogananda

and restlessness. It's where your mind is clear, and your body is completely calm and relaxed. This is when your thought processes become easily flowing and you can tap into the super-consciousness where all thoughts are formed.

You can liken it to a glass of water with a spoon of dirt mixed in and stirred. It quickly becomes cloudy with muddy water. But after a while, the mud settles down to the bottom of the glass when it is left to sit, and the water becomes clear again. The same happens with your thoughts after you remain quiet, sit still and motionless for a time. Your thinking is much clearer and focused, allowing you to think through your problems and issues, which allows your intuition to work better. Answers will come to you, as well as solutions to problems and issues, because you can think more calmly and clearly. Much focus and power can be brought to your thinking process when you reach this state. Your focus and concentration, like a muscle, become stronger the more you practice.

TIP 28: There is scientific proof that the practice of regular meditation changes us, not only our cell structures but our brain structures as well. One of the main benefits derived from regular meditation is the reduction of stress and cortisol, the hormone that works as a key player in the body's stress response. Cortisol is considered Public Enemy #1 by scientists who have known for years that elevated levels interfere with learning, memory, and immune function. It also increases risk for weight gain, high blood pressure, heart disease, depression, mental illness, and lower life expectancy.

The benefits derived from meditation are numerous. Once you make it part of your daily regimen, you'll wonder how you ever went through life without it. Because you will have found a port in the storm of life to escape when things get rough and tumultuous or even to start and end your day in a calm and centered place. Life becomes easier to deal with, so you can cope with life's day to day vicissitudes.

Daya Mata, former president of Self-Realization Fellowship, has said, "*Meditation helps us to align our outer life with the inner values of the soul as nothing else in this world can. It does not take away from family life or relationships with others. On the contrary, it makes us more loving, more understanding– it makes us want to serve our husband, our wife, our children, our neighbors. Real spirituality begins when we include others in our wish for well-being, when we expand our thoughts beyond 'I, me and mine.*"

She also said, "*Those who are able to schedule endless activities throughout the day, but not a few minutes with God, need to reevaluate their busyness. Their real problem is not lack of time, but an addiction to restlessness; and it is going to take more than simply using a new type of weekly calendar to cure it.*" and "*Most shun meditation not because they truly have no time, but because they do not want to face themselves– a definite result of the interiorization of meditation. The tragedy of complacency is that most persons do not begin to do something about bettering their spiritual condition until their hearts are wrung with torment, sadness, frustration, suffering. Only then do they turn toward seeking the Divine. Why wait and go through such anguish? It is so simple to feel God now if we make but a little effort in meditation.*"

Although meditation has been around for millennia, it has in the last couple of decades become more recognized by bio scientists as a life changing practice that people are finding and paying more attention to.

As our world has become more frenetic and tension-ridden, people are looking for ways to cope with the residual stress they carry with them throughout their daily lives. The escapism that many are seeking through alcohol, drugs, and other methods are just temporary fixes to the problem. Additionally, the temporary fixes come with long-term deleterious effects on those who persist in using them.

My habit of meditation has helped me throughout my adult life in all aspects. It has become such an ingrained part of my daily routine that I can't even conceive of not doing it after 35+ years of continuous practice. It would be like not brushing my teeth.

Once you establish the habit of daily meditation, you'll find that life is easier to cope with and handle, especially when you hit the trying times that test your mettle, which life inevitably presents to us at various times. You will have at your disposal a skillset that will carry you through whatever life brings you. The reason is that you will have connected your life with the Source of all there is.

The meditation I practice is Kriya Yoga. The Sanskrit word Yoga means union with God. Kriya Yoga was brought to the West by Paramahansa Yogananda from India back in 1920. He founded Self-Realization Fellowship, Church of All Religions, in Boston, where he first came to the United States. He taught the universality of all religions and the common goal of establishing a relationship with our Creator. Basically, his teachings state that we're all children of God and there's no reason to disrespect others' beliefs in God, because there are many paths that lead to Him.

His book, the spiritual classic, *Autobiography of a Yogi,* which has sold millions, has been heralded as one of the top 100 books on spirituality in the past century. It is required reading in many universities around the world on the subject of Eastern religion.

The documentary film, *Awake: The Life of Yogananda*, personalizes his own quest for enlightenment and sharing his struggles along the path. Yogananda made ancient Vedic teachings accessible to a modern audience, attracting many followers and inspiring the millions who practice yoga today.

Before he died, Steve Jobs, the late business visionary and founder of Apple Computer, requested that everyone who attended his memorial service receive a small brown box containing a copy of *Autobiography of a Yogi*. According to Walter Isaacson's biography, Jobs first read the book as a teenager, then reread it in India and once a year ever since. It was the only book he had on his iPad.

"*You would be hard-pressed to find anyone on the spiritual path whose life has not been influenced by this profound work of litera-ture,*" states bestselling author Jack Canfield, co-creator of the super-successful, *Chicken Soup for the Soul* series and whose own personal spiritual journey was influenced by reading, *Autobiography of a Yogi.*

The book has had a profound effect on many influential people and on people all over the world from different religions and all walks of life.

George Harrison of The Beatles was one who encouraged others to read the book and gave away dozens of copies throughout his life. He had his good friend, Ben Kingsley, the Academy Award winning actor, narrate the audiobook which can be found on iTunes or Audible.com, where he makes it come to life.

I've been an avid reader my entire life. No other book has had such a major positive influence upon me. It changed my life when I first read it as a young man of 18. Yogananda explained that each of us can have a personal relationship with our creator. Who could be closer to us than He who knows us better than we know ourselves? He also says that unless and until we prove it to ourselves, we may want to believe and even say we believe, but we won't truly believe it. He states that you don't have to change your religion to come to this understanding. In fact, you'll be even more devout in your religion than you were before you proved it to yourself.

As I read *Autobiography of a Yogi*, I kept coming across truths that hit me, like a tuning fork being struck inside me. I would say to myself, "I always knew that that was true," like I was having an epiphany. Yogananda says that that is your soul recognizing what it has always known.

I have given many of copies of the book away to others in my life. Practically everybody I've spoken to who has read it told me it was one of the most profound spiritual books they ever read.

Once you read or listen to the book you will have a clearer understanding of the practice of meditation. You will also have a greater perspective of the universality of religion, as you come to the realization and understanding that all the major religions are working to get to the common goal of reaching God.

ACTION ITEMS

- ✔ Give meditation a try by trying a guided meditation on the www.yogananda-srf.org website or some other technique you may find.

- ✔ Give it a 30-day trial period of at least once a day for 5-10 minutes either in the morning first thing or at night before going to sleep. If you do it daily, you will begin to feel and experience some of the benefits discussed.

- ✔ Read or listen to *Autobiography of a Yogi* to get the foundational understanding of yoga to learn why and how it benefits you. I promise you will not be disappointed.

Chapter 16

INSPIRE OTHERS, ALWAYS!

This is a universal law that continues to reward those who are quick to provide inspiration and encouragement when confronted by those who need it. They also receive the encouragement and inspiration they are offering to others. As I like to say, "We need reminding as much as we need learning."

The promise of this universal law is that when you have this concept as part of your mindset, you can't help but inspire yourself as well as others.

> "I don't know what your destiny will be, but one thing I know: the only ones among you who will be really happy are those who will have sought and found how to serve."
> – Albert Schweitzer

I remember first hearing this idea taught during a seminar I attended when I was about 25. As the speaker explained how this works, it made perfect sense. Then, when I incorporated it into my own mindset, I saw the magic of it and how it affects others when I've inspired or encouraged them. Sometimes, the effect is far beyond what we ever know or realize.

I'm sure all of us at some point in life have been inspired by someone's kind words of encouragement. Sometimes there are words of inspiration imparted to us at difficult times in our life when we really needed to hear it, essentially giving us the impetus necessary to make a greater effort towards a goal or objective we felt unsure about. It may have been just the words we needed at the time in order to help us over the hill of our lack of self-confidence or discouragement.

It's been said that sometimes all we need to accomplish great things is to have someone who believes in us more than we do in ourselves and encourages us to take the leap of faith necessary. I've been fortunate to have teachers, mentors, and parents who have encouraged and inspired me through-out my life. If you have not had the same benefit, make sure you are the one inspiring and encouraging others. I promise you will not only benefit from it, but you will be rewarded exponentially.

Ways you can inspire others:
- **Inspire others by expecting the most of them**. Most of us will rise to the expectations of the people who believe in us. Find reasons to believe in the people around you and communicate your high expectations. Encourage them and let them know that you have faith that they will achieve what they set out to do.
- **Inspire others by challenging them**. While you are communicating your faith in the people around you, help them raise the bar as well. Encourage them to try new things and confront new obstacles they haven't faced before. Doing so will make them stronger and increase their faith in themselves.
- **Inspire others by showing that you care about them**. Expectations and challenges won't matter much unless you are also authentically caring about the people you're hoping to inspire.

- **Inspire others by having the courage to change course**. Even as you stay true to what you believe in, be sure to remain flexible. A true leader doesn't hold rigidly to a path he or she has chosen in the past when that path turns out to be the wrong one.
- **Inspire others by being vulnerable**. Be honest about who you are and your own shortcomings and failures. People are much more apt to follow and be inspired by someone who presents as a real human being than someone who seems too good to be true. Talk about the obstacles and difficulties you've overcome and demonstrate that it is possible to remain strong and resilient in the face of difficult times.
- **Inspire others by practicing integrity**. Speak the truth, even if it's not what someone wants to hear. Avoid gossip and attacks on others. Rise above petty politics and be someone people count on to do the right thing.
- **Inspire others by sharing the credit**. A leader shares success and is someone other people want to follow and even emulate.
- **Inspire others by sharing your influences**. Talk about the people who have inspired you. Tell stories of the people who have impacted your life. The more people hear about others who have achieved meaning and success, the more they will believe that they can do so themselves.

ACTION ITEMS

- ✔ Start making a conscious effort to inspire others when the opportunity presents itself.
- ✔ Practice being inspirational and motivating others with your own stories and experiences of when you overcame personal obstacles and difficulties.

✔ Let others know that they can overcome all obstacles
   with the right attitude and determination. Share
   encouraging words to help them, whether it be through
   a favorite quote of yours or by recommending a book
   that you believe will help inspire and motivate them.

Chapter 17

MAKE SERVICE YOUR GOAL

Making service your main goal when working for others is a transformational mindset you need to adopt. Many of you may already have this as your approach to helping others in your profession, job, or previous work. If so, that's fantastic. This comes naturally to you. For those who haven't instilled this as your mindset while working, you will want to. The benefits are extraordinary, and you will be setting a universal law in action that is beneficial to you and all involved.

First, the people you are serving will immediately feel that you have their best interests in mind rather than your compensation, commission,

> "Make service your goal rather than money, and you will see the entire cause-effect principle of your life change. You will never be left out again. When we act solely to benefit ourselves, such selfishness limits our consciousness, constricting the opening through which true prosperity and joy flow into our lives. If you do this, undreamed of power and happiness will come to you."
>
> – Paramahansa Yogananda

or payment when the service is rendered or the product is delivered. That's because they will hear the questions you are asking, your demeanor and your approach to trying to serve them will demonstrate that you have their interests in mind first. This cannot be faked. You must be genuine in your desire to help and serve them. Otherwise, it will come across as disingenuous and hollow.

It takes all the tension out of the process and allows the client or customer to relax and be more receptive to what you're trying to help them with. Granted, there will be those who are naturally skeptical and wary of others who are trying to sell them something.

If you are sincere in your efforts to give them the best service you have to offer, with their best interests in mind, they'll soon pick up on that and respond accordingly. Your job is to do just that and let the rest happen.

Especially in today's new economy, this will play a big part in who will win the business. People are smart. They can tell if you're in it just to make a few bucks and move on. Most likely they will pass on you and move to the next vendor or service provider.

Remember the saying, *"People don't care how much you know until they know how much you care."* It's never been truer and carries more weight than ever in today's world. Once you convey that in a way that makes them feel as though you are interested in helping them and care about their needs, they'll be much more willing to listen to what you have to say.

When you set this universal law in action you open the way for prosperity to come to you. It seems natural because it is, and it's a major game-changer. If you go to a store or are dealing with a vendor or businessperson who is trying to sell you something and not paying attention to your needs, it becomes obvious. They're not interested so much in your needs as much as selling you something. It's a turn-off, and we don't want to deal with them.

Putting this universal law into effect will be one of the single greatest moves you can do to enhance your business. Its ripple effect impacts your life in so many positive ways.

ACTION ITEMS

- ✔ Make service your goal whenever you're dealing with others.

- ✔ Think of ways you can remind yourself to serve others, either by post-it notes near your desk or on your mobile phone's home screen.

- ✔ Remind yourself before you go to a meeting or approach a prospective client, "How can I provide them with excellent service?"

Chapter 18

SPIRITUALIZING BUSINESS: THE KEY THAT UNLOCKS YOUR PROSPERITY & HAPPINESS

Throughout the ages, all of the great saints and sages have espoused that spiritualizing business is the way to find prosperity and happiness. You'll find this common thread runs throughout all of the major religions. When you approach life with *love and service* uppermost in mind, you'll see the entire cause–effect principle change it for the better. People perceive you from a different perspective because they feel you're looking after their best interests. Your entire demeanor and approach to your

> *"Both material and spiritual success should be obtained. Material success consists in possessing the necessities of life. Ambition for money-making should include a desire to help others. Acquire all the money you can by improving in some way your community or country or the world, but never seek financial gain by acting against their interests."*
> - Paramahansa Yogananda

business and relationships, as well as everything in your life shows it. Prosperity is attracted to those who are working for others' prosperity and benefit.

Let's talk about prosperity for a moment. What defines prosperity, and how do we evaluate it? Prosperity means the ability to provide for yourself and your loved ones the necessities of life. This may refer to myriad aspects of modern-day life. For you, it may mean a new home with new furnishings, a new car, a new wardrobe, a bank account with a years' worth of expenses covered, your kids' education covered, etc. For another person, it may mean a mansion with an ocean view, a new Rolls Royce, $50 million in the bank, etc. There are a multitude of people in the world who look at prosperity as a roof over their head, food on the table, and furniture in their home with running water and toilets. Essentially, it's all relative. Here in the USA, most of us are fortunate enough to be able to obtain whatever we can dream of having, if we are willing to work for it.

The interesting thing is that most people here, when asked to make a list of everything they want or could have, only come up with maybe five or six things. When pressed, they may be able to squeeze three to four more things onto the list. Then, when you ask them to define each item in terms of monetary value put on them, it will usually come up with a number that is reachable for them.

Our needs are few and our wants are endless, at times. The problem for most of us is we don't know exactly what we want.

If you put some thought to many of the items you have longed for, decided to go after, and obtained, you would see that the joy of owning them starts to wain after a short time. The object loses its luster and the novelty wears off. Soon, you're off looking at another item, a newer version, the latest gadget, or whatever else you think is going to bring you more happiness in your life. That's just the way the world works.

If we keep seeking happiness outside of ourselves in the objects or goals we're seeking, we'll continue to be disappointed after a while. Happiness is elusive. Mainly because it's a byproduct of serving others and trying to make others happy. When you're seeking it directly, it seems to be ever evasive. When serving God by serving others, you feel the effects of happiness because you're not looking for it for yourself. The irony is, if you realize that serving others makes you happy, then in a way, you are serving yourself. You will continue to be disappointed if you are seeking it directly. It's an inside job. I'm sure you must have heard the saying, "If you're feeling unhappy, go out and try to make someone else happy by serving them in some way." Try it sometime. You'll discover for yourself how effective it is.

We need to learn how to *surrender* our lives to God in order to receive all the blessings He has for us. Many times, we're fortunate not to receive the things we wished and hoped for. He knows what is best for us. When we let Him choose, we will get that which is for our highest good. He'll pick what's best for us, but we must trust.

Surrender is about doing our best but trusting the outcome to God and not becoming attached to it.

TIP 29: There is a video on YouTube by Oprah Winfrey called "Surrender". It's a perfect example of what I'm talking about here. Check it out. I got goosebumps when I watched it. I had to watch it again after I saw it the first time. It's a super powerful testimonial of the power of surrender.

You need to remind yourself that "God's delays are not God's denial," as Robert Schuller, the late author and minister of the famous Crystal Cathedral in Orange County, California, would say. Sometimes there are reasons, unknown to us, as to why God wants us to exercise our patience muscles before we receive certain things in our life. I can think of numerous examples in my life, and you probably can too if you think about it.

The important thing to remember is to stay attuned to your spiritual purpose of serving God by consistently serving others until it becomes a habit that is unshakable. Once you establish that kind of habit, you'll see your entire world transformed.

Chapter 19

BECOME A LIFELONG LEARNER

There are many benefits to derive from becoming a lifelong learner. I believe that in the new economy it is a necessity to always be learning. Things are changing so rapidly that it's difficult to keep up with new ideas and ways of conducting business without continuously learning the latest innovations and trends in your business. It's also good to know what new services and skills people are looking for and where you can add value for them.

The Japanese have a word for this philosophy: kaizen. It means change for the better, or continuous improvement. It's an approach of constantly introducing small incremental changes in business to improve quality and efficiency.

Unless and until we can prove that we can add value to the products or services our prospective customers or clients are looking for, we're going to struggle with the masses in trying to earn a living. That will only become more difficult with time. It's better to be ahead of the curve, by offering the best possible service or benefit for the client. You can only do that if you are on the cutting edge of your industry.

It's easy to become a learning machine if you instill some of the habits we've discussed, such as listening to podcasts in your respective industry, listening to audiobooks, and reading periodicals, magazines, newsletters, and books related to your and other businesses.

TIP 30: It is a good practice to learn about what others do in their industries and see how you can apply their tips, strategies, and tactics to your industry or business. It's surprising what you can find out from others who are not in your industry by soliciting their opinions and perspectives about yours. It can be enlightening. We tend to get into a thinking rut when it comes to our own businesses.

If you're constantly looking for and seeking out new information to add value to your customers or clients, you're bound to uncover gems from time to time to bring your business to another level. That should be your goal. If you're looking for it, you'll somehow find it.

It's refreshing when you meet others who conduct their business that way, mainly because they're a rare breed. That's what makes them valuable and sought after by others. They look at things differently and are constantly working at improving themselves and their business. Those who conduct business with them are getting value above and beyond what the market is usually offering. People today want more "bang for their buck", and they're willing to pay for it. Sometimes a lot more. Why? Because those who provide exceptional service or products are hard to find and the people who do find them are happy to discover them.

If you go out and compete on price you end up in a race to the bottom. Those who are looking for a bargain will generally settle for less if it means a lower price. They'll sacrifice quality and service. But you do get what you pay for. That's why the lowest price bid is not always the best way to go. You will end up paying more for it somewhere, in quality of service, by being charged more if you want it done right, or by having to pay someone else do it over again.

ACTION ITEMS

- ✔ Generate different ways you can improve what you're doing or planning on doing, that will separate you from the competition.

- ✔ Start the process today of becoming the best at what you do or provide. It may be studying new techniques, processes, or systems. It can be enrolling in a course or buying a program, or even hiring a coach to give you some pointers for improvement.

- ✔ Remember the concept of kaizen and start implementing it for yourself and your business.

Chapter 20

NAVIGATING THE NEW ECONOMY

The internet was for the modern world what the printing press was to the old world in the fifteenth century. It changed everything. The difference is that the internet propelled progress at warp speed and is continuing to do so. In our lifetimes, we have witnessed more and faster changes than any preceding generation. It's safe to say we'll continue to see massive technological change that will impact our lives in multiple ways.

The best part about the internet is that it leveled the playing field for many industries and for us as individual workers in many businesses. The challenge it has created is a vast ocean of businesses and people all looking to be heard or recognized among the masses.

What does that mean for you and me? It means we better be able to differentiate ourselves from others, so we can get the attention we need that allows us to use our skillsets to serve others in our businesses and industries.

As explained in the previous chapter, first and foremost, we must develop our abilities so that we can be good at what we do before we can serve others. That means constantly honing our skills and talents so that we can offer excellent service and exceed others' expectations in what we do. In other words, we must constantly be sharpening the saw.

Our world is moving so quickly now that continuous learning is no longer an option, but a necessity. People want more value from service providers, businesses, and anything they're paying their hard-earned money for. They will scour reviews online and scrutinize everything to the nth degree before moving forward with hiring or purchasing what they need.

There are certain things that remain constant and require us to be adept at. One very important human quality for business, and in every aspect of life for that matter, is communication. How we communicate with others has a huge effect on how we get along in life.

Specifically, for our purposes, I'm talking about marketing communication. Today, more than ever, we need to become proficient in how we market and communicate with others about our services, businesses, products, industry, etc.

There are five skills I would advise any young person in college starting out in today's business world to master. They are marketing, writing, public speaking, sales, and teamwork. In the next five chapters, I'll explain these skills and why they are critical for today's economy.

It's never too late to learn these skills. To elevate your knowledge base for getting ahead in the new economy, these skills will serve you in any income producing occupation you decide to accelerate in. The quicker you can learn and become proficient in these abilities, the better you will be able to help others.

Marketing

Marketing has always been an important skill to learn and possess. The challenge today is that people have limited attention spans and will quickly dismiss anyone who doesn't immediately grab their attention in the first five seconds or less. We are bombarded with literally thousands of marketing messages each day on the internet, smartphones, television, radio or podcasts, billboards, newspapers, and magazines. All of them are vying for our attention. It's no wonder our brains want to filter out most of these messages.

Sales

Whether you want to believe it or not, we are all in sales. It is an essential skill that will continue to reward you for your efforts at becoming skillful at it. The profession of selling has changed dramatically over the years. It has progressed more to educating your prospect or customer and helping them to make informed and intelligent decisions, based on your ability to discern exactly what their needs are and then help them with that information. We'll discuss it in more detail and how to get better at it.

Writing

We all write every day in some form or fashion. Whether it's in a text, email or some other written form. What is important is not so much what we say, but how we express ourselves and what words we use. That can make a huge difference in how our communication affects people.

Speaking

Like writing and marketing, the way we speak and how we convey our messaging will make the difference between having someone do what we want and having them ignore us. That involves more than just words. Studies have proven that much of our verbal communication is not words primarily, but the tonality and body language that accompanies the words. Since we are in a world that is used to seeing their messaging on video in conferencing, YouTube, advertisements, and teaching, we must learn how to do this effectively.

Teamwork

You can't expect to move forward with the same velocity that you would if you have others helping you along the way. In today's world it is imperative that you learn to work with others if you want to achieve great things. It's not always easy if you've been working as a solopreneur most of your career. It's critical to learn because of the many benefits to be derived from teamwork. You can't possibly be all things, at all times. It's not very efficient, and you're short-changing yourself by not allowing teamwork to become part of what you offer.

Once you begin to master these five essential skills, you will be able to excel in just about any business environment.

Chapter 21

MARKETING: LEARN HOW TO TURN WORDS INTO GOLD

Marketing and sales go hand-in-hand. Sales has always been one of those subjects that has a negative connotation for some people. This is mainly because there are some shady individuals and companies that try to use marketing to draw unwary customers in to take advantage of them. However, you must be able to attract the clients and customers that you want and need so that they will buy whatever service or product you have to offer.

As I mentioned before, it has become harder than ever to grab others' attention when it comes to marketing. That's why it is important to become not just proficient but excellent at it. Fortunately, there are many resources out there to help you do just that.

Whether you're planning to do more web-based advertising or print, once you learn this skill, it is easily transferrable to other mediums. You will most likely be doing both anyway, as well as video and speaking. It's important to view this skillset as a tool to help you in all areas of the business you decide you want to be in. It's not just for marketing but for whatever you're trying to get others to do or be motivated by.

TIP 31: I would suggest you start with a copy writing course, of which there are many good ones out there. One of the copy writing courses I found to be of excellent help is offered by Digital Marketer (www.digitalmarketer.com). They feature several excellent courses on the various aspects of digital marketing. I have taken numerous courses from them, all of which have been valuable.

Digital marketing in general is in a constant state of flux and changes all the time. That's why you need to stay abreast of what's new. If you don't, you eventually find out you're wasting your time, money, and energy by going down the wrong road with your marketing efforts.

There's much to learn about where your service or product is most likely to find ready, willing, and able clients and customers. It's an inexact science at best, but there are ways to help pinpoint where it makes the most sense to spend your money. The more you learn and know about marketing, the easier it will be to determine where your customers and clients hang out and where and how to reach them.

I've worked with many digital marketers in my businesses. Some good, some not so good. You should know that it's very rare to find a marketer that has both marketing savvy and expertise in the technical end of digital marketing. Some claim they do, but I have not come across any really good ones yet. Some talk a good game and lead you to believe they can do it all. I've learned the hard way and paid a lot of money for little results. My website looked good, but it didn't attract the business I was hoping to get with the marketing strategy they sold me on.

I've learned that marketers who are completely honest about their skill sets will tell you that they do the marketing end but can't execute the technical side. Sometimes they will recommend a technical expert and other times you'll have to find one yourself, which is not too difficult to do.

TIP 32: You can find excellent freelance digital marketers and technical website experts on the myriad of sites where you can solicit bids for help from all over the world. I've had graphic artists from Pakistan design my logos, and others from Singapore, Canada, and other countries design my book covers. I've mentioned a couple of resources already, such as www.Freelancer.com and www.guru.com, but there are plenty of others like www.99designs.com. At the back of this book I have several resources listed that can assist you with a variety of tasks and services, so you don't have to look very far.

If you make becoming an expert in marketing a top priority, it will pay huge dividends in the years to come. The payback will be exponential compared to the time spent in learning and honing your skills in the field.

I constantly look for books, audiobooks, articles, podcasts, and videos that spotlight new and proven marketing strategies and tips. This has helped immensely with my businesses. You'll find it to be fun and exciting when you discover something new that works for your product or service.

My intent with this book is to give you an overview of what strategies and directions work and what I have found to be effective. Marketing is a vast subject that I couldn't even attempt to start to expound on because it contains so many different facets. I do know that you want to be skillful at it and make it part of your regular educational program.

ACTION ITEMS

✔ Make it a top priority to become an expert at marketing. Go on Digitalmarketer.com today and order their copy writing course. That would be an excellent start and foundation builder to begin your marketing efforts.

✔ Start your learning process by reading and listening to marketing audiobooks and podcasts. There are many available that are excellent and will help you jump-start your marketing. **Marketing Over Coffee**, **Call to Action**, and **Marketing School** are a few of them.

✔ *Influence: The Psychology of Persuasion* by Robert Cialdini is a classic for marketers to read. Seth Godin's books on marketing are also very good. There are many other excellent books out there. If you read or listened to one a month for two years, you would become a proficient marketer and a marketing expert.

✔ Never stop learning about marketing, and continuously test your marketing efforts to see which work the best for you. You never know which one will take you to the next level.

Chapter 22

SALES: THE CRITICAL SKILL TO TURBO-CHARGE YOUR EARNING POWER

Sales and marketing are similar in the respect that you are selling your ideas, products or services with both. Marketing is the medium you use to attract those individuals, companies or organizations to focus on what you are offering. Sales is the art of selling them through your words, concepts, processes and psychological approaches to consummate a sale.

Our world is changing more rapidly than ever before and requires us to be more adaptable than ever. I believe we're all in sales. Whether it's selling our spouse on where we want to go on vacation, out to eat or selling our boss on why we deserve a raise.

For many, selling yourself and your own services or products may feel way too far out of your comfort zone. Like anything else in life, the more we expose ourselves to it, the easier and less scary it becomes. As humans, we're wired that way. We must desensitize ourselves to those things we are afraid or unwilling to do because of self-preservation or fear of failure.

Sales requires us to interact and talk with those we don't know. The interesting thing about it is that most people are generally friendly and won't scream at you for contacting them. It's really all in your approach. Remember my advice on love and service. It diffuses most of the anxiety and people's hesitation and negative reactions to you contacting them. Yes, you will occasionally run into those who are having a bad day or are generally miserable. But most are not, and you can't take the reactions of others who aren't friendly personally. They don't even know you, so there's no reason to. Eventually you will not even worry about it after you start contacting people to discuss your product or services.

The bestselling author Jeb Blount is among the best sales trainers I've come across in all my years in sales. His books and training programs are top notch and are some of the most popular out there.

Here are notes I've taken from his best-selling book, *Fanatical Prospecting*, that you can apply to any sales scenario:
- Asking is the beginning of receiving!
- You must constantly ask for what you want confidently, assertively, and regularly.
- When you ask confidently and assertively, prospects will respond in kind.
- Allow prospects to talk about themselves. You'll find out much more if you ask open-ended questions; wait four to five seconds, and practice deep listening.
- #1-Ask confidently and assume you're going to get it!
- #2-Shut up! No matter how long it takes for them to respond.
- #3-Get ready for any objections!
- Accept a lack of response as a good thing. Get objections on the table early and often to determine if you have a real prospect.
- Start constructing your scripts for your five most common objections. That way you'll be prepared. After

two buyer objections, back off graciously. Get back to them another time.

- You must have a plan when prospecting. Don't say, "I was just reaching out…" or, "That's great!" If you don't have a plan you will come off as just another salesperson spewing the typical phrases your prospect has heard repeatedly. Their minds will tune you out and most likely you'll be shut down.
- You must seek out rejection and make yourself stronger, so your esteem becomes more powerful.
- You must learn to be rejection-proof when speaking to prospects.
- Determine early on whether the person you're dealing with can make the necessary decisions. Do this by asking who else is involved in making the decisions to move forward and whether they can walk you through the process.
- Get to "no" fast! They're doing you a favor if they have no intention of doing business with you. DON'T take it personally.
- Remember, yes always has a number. Meaning, be polite, be patient and be persistent. No does not necessarily mean never. It just means they're not ready now. If you believe they are a good prospect, keep in touch with them and develop a stronger rapport.
- Never ever leave a prospecting call without discussing next steps.
- Live by the mantra: "One more call!"

Apply this to all sales efforts when prospecting for customers. Learning to sell and be resilient will pay off huge dividends for those willing to apply these principles and their efforts.

TIP 33: If you add sales to your list of things to become proficient in, you'll be miles ahead of any competition you face out there. Most people in sales never even pick up a book on selling or consider studying their craft. In the new economy, I consider it a must. If you choose to ignore it, you'll find it more difficult to move forward and gain traction. You'll be surprised by how it will help you in so many other areas of your work and life.

ACTION ITEMS

✔ Commit to start getting outside of your comfort zone by doing those things you thought you could not do. You'll experience a new way of life you'll find exciting.

✔ Think about how to become good at sales. It will help you in your efforts to start a new income stream or get your business generating more income. Then implement your new skills by targeting new customers and prospects.

✔ Study sales programs and listen to audiobooks on selling. I highly recommend Jeb Blount's books and programs.

Chapter 23

WRITING: THE ESSENTIAL SKILL YOU NEVER STOP PRACTICING

If you learn to write properly, you'll find that your thoughts start to crystallize on the computer or paper in a manner that becomes easier the more you do it. Why is this important? You will be the one, most of the time, putting forth your ideas, your commentaries, your arguments, and your persuasions. Since we live in a world of soundbites, where people want information in as few words as possible, it's imperative that you know how to communicate as effectively and cogently as possible.

No doubt, you've heard the expression, "If I had more time, I would have written a shorter letter." The goal is to write in the most effective way possible with the least amount of words. It's not an easy task, but if you constantly work at it, it starts to come more naturally.

Since we all use the various communications that require our writing skills to be exercised, such as texting, email, business and personal letters, Twitter, etc., it is important that we convey our thoughts clearly.

It's amazing how some people don't even think twice about sending an email out without reviewing it first. Riddled with typos, grammatical errors, and bad structure, these emails reflect poorly on the sender. I get that we've all made some of those mistakes at some point due to our rushing or being distracted, but it sends a bad message (pardon the pun). It says that the sender doesn't really care about the recipient or about whatever it is that they are selling, promoting, or saying in their email. Take the time to review your words and correct errors. It can make the difference between having someone interested enough respond to your email and having people deleting your message because of its unprofessionalism.

When I hear people lament that they don't know how to write well or were never very good at it in school, I tell them that it's not a skill that you're born with. It's a learned skill, and like any other skill, the more you do it, the better you get at it. Plus, there are so many tools today to help us with our writing, including spelling and grammar checks.

TIP 34: Obtain a book on writing and learn what it takes to develop the skill. Also, practice your grammar skills. One of the best books out there is a classic and has been around for ages. It is Strunk and White's, *The Elements of Style*, a small book that's all instruction on proper grammar and structure. It is super helpful and instructional in writing properly, so you can sound like a professional and a learned scholar (but not seem pompous).

There are plenty of programs, podcasts, and audiobooks available that can help you develop writing ability. Nothing is better or can replace practicing writing consistently. If you read and write regularly, you'll find it less of a task than if you do it periodically.

Try writing articles about your field of expertise. These essays can run anywhere from 500 to 1000 words. It's an excellent way to start becoming proficient at your writing skills and using them in your marketing efforts. Post your articles to LinkedIn, Facebook Ads, periodicals, trade magazines, websites, etc. After writing 25 to 30 articles, you can compile them into a book that you can publish. Look into ezinearticles. com, where you'll find loads of ideas, formats, and how-to information.

> **TIP 35:** You can also put together *special reports* to use as a marketing or lead magnet to get others to sign up on your website. This is a value-added document that you offer for free on your website. Have site visitors opt in with their email address to download the report, then market your information to them using an email marketing list that you create. Remember, you're building a fan base, and those who are interested in getting your information will most likely want to get more from you.

The other helpful part of writing articles in your field of expertise is that it helps raise your credibility as an expert. You'd be surprised how much people appreciate the fact that you've had articles published. Put your contact information and your website URL at the bottom of your article and offer a complimentary copy of your special report or whatever else you may be able to give to them in order to get them to contact you.

Work at it and you will see progress. This action will pay you back exponentially for any time you spend improving it.

ACTION ITEMS

- ✔ Get yourself a book or audiobook on writing. You will find it motivating and it will spur you to start writing. Like anything else, the more you do it, the easier it gets.

- ✔ Look for podcasts that are helpful with your writing skills. The are many out there including **Grammar Girl** and **The Writer Files**.

✔ Set aside time to write daily. This can be for a journal or a project you set out to accomplish. Make it easy to establish the habit. Do it in the same place at the same time for the same amount of time each day.

Chapter 24

SPEAKING: TRANSFORM YOUR CAREER AND PERSONAL LIFE

Public speaking is the one skill that I promise will take your professional and personal life to a new level. The funny thing is that it's one of the most feared skills. People are petrified of public speaking. But like anything else in life, *face your fears and your fears will disappear.*

I can totally relate to this fear because I once was terrified by the prospect of getting up and speaking before a group of strangers. I lived through one of my most dreaded nightmares. I had to give a talk in a class I was enrolled in. There were about 75 people in attendance. When it was my turn to speak, I went in front of the class and was struck by a panic attack.

As I read my notated 3x5 cards, a drop of sweat rolled off my forehead, down the tip of my nose onto my cards. I started sweating like a farm animal. My entire shirt became drenched in a matter of minutes. I was humiliated and embarrassed. If that wasn't bad enough, my teacher asked me to pass out some papers for him when I was finished. I tried hard not to sweat too much on the papers and students as I handed them out. I felt like I was being punished for being so nervous. I felt embarrassed and humiliated.

I vowed as I was driving home that I would never put myself through that ever again. I was at a friend's party about three weeks later and was talking with his stepfather about my ordeal. He asked me a question that changed my view of public speaking.

> *"Have you ever heard of Toastmasters? It's an organization where people go and learn how to speak in public. The great thing about it is everyone goes there for the same reason. Very supportive and comfortable setting to learn in. I've been involved for many years. I can't recommend it more highly."*

I wanted to learn more about it. He told me to call the headquarters in San Diego (pre-internet days) to locate a chapter in my area. I found one that had just recently been established and decided to join.

I met some incredibly supportive and nice people there. I started to become used to standing up and speaking in front of others. It's scientifically proven that you become immune to fear and anxiety once you put yourself in the position that creates it and see that nothing bad happens.

About eight months after joining Toastmasters, I was asked by one of our large corporate client account executives if my partner and I would be willing to give a full day seminar to one of their departments. The thought at first struck me with trepidation. But, of course, we said yes, because it was an opportunity too good to pass up. We ended up presenting the seminar to about 50 attendees and earning seven assignments from the group, which was beyond our highest hopes.

Other benefits you'll derive from Toastmasters: increased self-confidence; better listening skills; ability to think on your feet and speak spontaneously; ability to organize your thoughts in an orderly fashion so that what you say is clear and effective.

Also, as they say in Toastmasters, "Teach the butterflies in your stomach to fly in formation when speaking in public."

I can't tell you how much it has impacted my personal life since my confidence level went right up. I'll be forever grateful for the lessons I learned by attending Toastmaster meetings.

The thing I enjoyed most from attending those meetings is the transformation of personalities I observed in fellow members. I witnessed people during their early meetings freeze in terror, unable to speak when they stood up to address the group, and then, less than six months later, they were giving impressive speeches. I saw how they carried themselves differently, with much more confidence. You can't buy this kind of change, but you can obtain it by embracing the uncomfortable and taking the challenge head-on.

TIP 36: Life begins outside of your comfort zone. Things that challenge you, change you. You need to get yourself outside of your comfort zone and into your stretch zone to experience it for yourself. Once you do, the next time will become a little easier. So will the next time after that, and so on until you'll welcome those opportunities, when they're presented, to stretch your comfort zone. You will feel empowered by overcoming your self-imposed limitations and will want to continue doing so.

This skill is one that will also elevate your credibility as you get up in front of others and speak confidently and cogently on your subject. This vital ability also applies to video recordings, online conference calls, YouTube recordings, etc. People will assume you're an expert in your subject because you have the confidence to stand up before a group and speak.

I can't recommend this enough to you if you truly want to transform your world and your career. This one move on your part will increase your abilities in so many other areas, it's too important not to do it. Others who have done it will confirm that it's true. Warren Buffet says developing this one skill can increase your net worth by 50%.

It's the best single skill I've acquired that has helped me the most in my career. Learn this and it will catapult yours.

ACTION ITEMS

- ✔ Go online today and look up Toastmasters International at Toastmasters.org to locate your local clubs. Choose two or three groups and find out when their meetings are.

- ✔ Attend each one of those club meetings at least once. The idea is to find one that you connect with most. If none of those work, keep searching until you find the one that does. It will be a major game-changer for you when you find it.

Chapter 25

TEAMWORK: A KEY COMPONENT TO GROW YOUR BUSINESS

S ome of us are used to getting things done on our own with little or no assistance when it comes to what we're good at. This is especially true for those who have been solopreneurs for most of their careers. I've been guilty of that myself. That changed for me when I went on a self-development adventure trip designed to help people understand how business and personal development can be catapulted by implementing the correct skills and mindset.

On the surface, it seemed quite rudimentary when it was explained to us. We were out in the wilderness of British Columbia, Canada, about 40 miles west of Whistler. This is one of the most beautiful natural settings I've ever been in. We were camping out for five days, and each day included some physical and mental training sessions that started at 6 a.m. and generally ended around midnight but sometimes later.

I experienced a paradigm shift through a program we had one day that required our team to undergo a series of grueling exercises including walking on a wire between trees about 15 feet off the ground and navigate to the other side (yes, we had a harness) while working our way around obstacles.

Another was climbing up a series of platforms made from two-by-four boards, about four feet apart, hanging from two constantly moving ropes tied to tree limbs about 25 feet off the ground. We each had a partner who was to help us get to the top. Below, two people were allowed to stabilize the platform boards by each holding a rope attached to either side of it.

It was one of the most difficult exercises we went through that day. It took all the strength I had, as well as patience. My partner, who was a big guy in the military, was having a difficult time balancing and getting up to each platform. We decided that I should be the one to get up to the next level first, then help him because he was having a tough time of it. He weighed at least 50 pounds more than me. We did make it to the top but not without supreme effort from both of us.

There were several other exercises we underwent that day that were also grueling. At the end of the session, we sat down to discuss what we learned from the experience. Unanimously, we all said you can do more than you think with the help of others.

Looking back, I can say that the exercises they put us through that day really drove that into my DNA. Before, I was guilty of trying to do many of my tasks and projects myself and only reaching out when I ran into something I couldn't figure out.

If you're going to grow your business, you're going to have to get used to the idea that it's not only OK to use other people's skills, it's necessary. There's really no reason not to since you can find reasonably priced experts in their fields from all over the world.

The ability to allow others to help us and join with us in a common objective is one that creates momentum that can't necessarily happen when one individual is going it alone. When you assemble a team of people working toward an objective, you've created a sum greater than the one mind. We can't be an expert in all things, nor can we be all things to all people. This one essential skill of allowing and enlisting others' help will be one of the greatest assists to your success in whatever your endeavors may be.

T-E-A-M: Together Everyone Achieves More.

ACTION ITEMS

✔ Put some thought as to where you can use help in your work and objectives. Then put out a job bid listing on one of the platforms we discussed earlier, such as upwork.com or freelancer.com.

✔ Make it a habit to think where you could use someone else's expertise in your projects, and then find out what it would cost once you receive bids. You may find it's much cheaper and efficient to hire it out.

✔ Commit to becoming a team builder and player. You'll find that the more you do it, the easier it becomes. The other benefit is that you're building your leadership skills.

Chapter 26

HIRE A COACH

One of the best things you can do for yourself if you're trying to master a skill or have reached a plateau in learning a skill, is to hire a coach. Someone who is an expert in the skill and is adept at teaching others how to master it.

When reading about high achievers and how they can master so many skills and achievements, a common secret many will divulge is that they hire a coach for each one. Whether it's for a sport, like tennis, skiing, or golfing, or some other goal. A coach can also help with speaking skills, presentations, organization, or for achieving all-around success. A digital marketing coach can help your ecommerce business or show you how to produce effective YouTube videos for your business. The list is endless, and there's a coach for just about everything you want to master. I would say it's the fast-track program to learning a skill, and nothing is quite

"The reason I've been able to be so financially successful is my focus has never, ever for one minute been money."

- Oprah Winfrey

like having an expert to help you on your journey to learning specific skills and tasks.

You need to decide how much you're willing to spend and how much time you must dedicate to learning the new skill. There are also different ways to engage a personal coach. Depending upon the skill, you could set up a regular call with them at a scheduled time each week or more often. You could have a video call to speak and see each other face-to-face. You can meet in-person at a specified time and place.

You could go through their video or in-person course, then have a one-on-one coaching session that you organize with them. You can go through each segment or module, then have a coaching call or session with them. Do video coaching calls with them.

I can tell you firsthand, the coaches I have hired to help me learn various skills over the years have been invaluable. Not all of them have been excellent, but most of them have been helpful to me in mastering certain aspects where I was having trouble grasping or getting over a hurdle I was struggling with. I would say it saved me, in some cases, years of frustrating trial and error lessons.

What always amazes me are the professional athletes, like Tiger Woods and Rafael Nadal, or even well-respected surgeons in their field who have professional coaches to help them be their best at what they do. Itzhak Perlman, a world-renowned concert violinist, has had a coach for over 40 years. Oftentimes it takes someone else to point out areas you can improve upon to get to another level. Never stop the pursuit of becoming better and more skillful at something. This lifelong pursuit keeps driving you toward excellence and keeps you motivated.

TIP 37: There are times when spending just a few hours with a coach can literally transform your skillset. Making a few suggestions for changes after observing you perform your skill can enlighten you to things you were unaware of. Many times it can be simple tweaks, but it's enough to make a positive difference.

We all have significant room for improvement in our lives. The question is, are you ready to confront this and allow a coach to help you reach new heights for your skillsets and yourself?

ACTION ITEMS

✔ Decide where you can gain advantage in learning or improving in an existing skill or a new skill by hiring a coach. Look into various ways you can implement a coaching program for it.

✔ Ask yourself if you're willing to give it a try and be honest with yourself. You must be open to coaching. If you have a problem with someone telling you what and how to do things, you need to get over that.

✔ Be sure to vet your prospective coaches so you trust them and feel comfortable about what they are saying they can do for you. Ask for references.

Chapter 27

WHY YOU SHOULD NEVER STOP WORKING ENTIRELY

There has been plenty of research on people who have re-tired from their jobs or careers only to find themselves dissatisfied with their retirement or even who pass away shortly after retiring. This is mainly because they have a lack of purpose for getting up in the morning. Their identities are so tied up in their work that they have difficulties recalibrating themselves to retirement because they hadn't developed any other interests or hobbies to keep themselves occupied

"Don't take life too seriously. You'll never get out of it alive."
- Elbert Hubbard

when they woke up with no place to go. Sure, some enjoy hobbies like golf, tennis, fishing, playing Bridge, or traveling. But that's not always enough to satisfy most people.

I've known friends and others who retired and told me they plan to watch over their stock portfolio or real estate holdings. What I've seen is many of them becoming anxious while watching over their stocks because of the constant market swings. Most stock experts agree that it's not a good practice to be scrutinizing your stock portfolio daily. You can end up making poor decisions based upon your emotions and the stock news of the day.

The point is that you need something other than keeping an eye on things to satisfy your need to feel productive. I know there's a time and a place to let go and enjoy yourself. That's fine for a finite amount of time for the majority of people. Then, most of us will become antsy and start looking for something else to do.

Unless we have constructive hobbies and activities to busy our minds, we have a tendency to see boredom and tedium slip in. Having a reason and purpose to get up each morning and be somewhere or do something allows us to feel like we have a purpose in our lives.

My father worked until age 87 and told me it had much to do in keeping him going and sticking around. His axiom is, "Stay active physically and mentally every day. It's the secret to longevity."

I always liked a statement made by Jack LaLanne, the fitness and nutrition television celebrity who passed away at age 96. He said, "It's easier to rust out than to wear out." He exercised for two hours every day, even on vacation. He also said, "It all comes back to one big lesson: Life never ends. As long as we're alive, we have to be constantly improving. We have to be constantly growing – and growth is often where we feel like life is fulfilling."

Scientists have discovered that exercising the body will continue to make it resilient and able to defy the aging process as we grow older. It allows us to have the immunity, muscle mass, and cholesterol levels of a young person.

Some of the most exciting news about exercising as we age is what it does for the brain. Exercise helps to keep brain cells healthy, keeps blood vessels delivering plenty of oxygen to the brain, enhances the connections to the brain cells, and may even help grow new brain cells.

We must keep our minds busy as well if we want our capacity to think at our optimal capability. We can do that by reading regularly, socializing with others, developing our interests in other subjects and outside activities that stimulate our brains. That can mean learning to play an instrument or helping others in some way by contributing time to a worthy cause or need.

Working part-time or even full-time can help to keep us feeling younger and keep our thinking capacities sharp.

TIP 38: Volunteering to help organizations or charities will give you a feeling of satisfaction in knowing you're contributing to their cause and is another way to keep your mind and body active in a productive manner. This works well for those who don't have the need or desire to generate more income. Your time, energy, and efforts will be much appreciated, and the payoff you receive will be a feeling of goodwill and peace of mind.

If you want to live a more fulfilling life, you must remain active both physically and mentally.

ACTION ITEMS

- ✔ Make a commitment to stay active throughout your life, and you'll reap the rewards of fulfillment until the end.

- ✔ Decide that there's always more to be interested in and more to get involved with in life.

- ✔ Remember, there's no such thing as a boring life, just boring people.

Chapter 28

HOW MUCH DO YOU NEED TO EARN TO LIVE A NICE LIFESTYLE?

This is a subjective question to get you to think about what you really believe you need in order to maintain a nice lifestyle. Our needs are few, but our wants are seemingly endless. The interesting thing about it is we probably could have a good lifestyle including some of those items and so-called luxuries that most people want in their lives, for much less than you may think.

The first thing we need to do is put together a list of what we would consider to be essential to live the lifestyle we want. Grab a sheet of paper or pull up a blank document on your computer and start your list.

It may include the following:

- Would you move to a different location other than where you're currently living? Is climate a determining factor for your location?
- Would you rent or buy your home?
- What do you consider necessary for your living standards? A gym or other fitness membership, a certain

number of meals out weekly, other entertainment such as plays or concerts, etc.?
- Would you keep a car or use public transportation?
- What would your monthly groceries cost you?
- How many vacations per year? Where and for how long? What type of accommodations would you require?
- What are your medical insurance needs? Are you paying your medical insurance yourself, through your employer, with Medicare, etc.?

Add other items you feel are a necessity for your desired lifestyle. Then, itemize the expense attached to each item.

Keep in mind that these expenses will vary according to where you choose to live. It could have a major impact on expenses, as we discussed earlier. The purpose of this exercise is to reveal what you desire for a nice lifestyle. Secondly, it allows you to think through the list and determine the importance of each aspect you have chosen as you do your cost-benefit analysis. Thirdly, you can rethink the list and its choices, and then determine how much you need to earn to maintain that lifestyle.

The interesting part of this is that when you sit down and list out your must-haves, you'll find that they are within your reach, once you know where the income will be generated from.

The person who knows what they want and is willing to put the thought and effort into making it happen will be more likely to make it happen. You can pay for whatever you feel is what you want to enjoy, assuming it's affordable for you. Whether that is a splurge on a first-class hotel stay or a meal at a top-rated restaurant. It's your money and you can spend it however you like. There can be a happy medium, so you feel like you're experiencing all the good things you want to.

TIP 39: Keep in mind that many times it's better to rent the things you want or even buy them used. I say that because I've been through the exercise of buying something I believed I had to have, and shortly after, I put it away and rarely, if ever, used it again. I now make myself wait 24 hours before making a purchase over $100 and three days if over $500. Often, I find I no longer feel I want or need it after the wait period.

ACTION ITEMS

✔ Go through the exercises and determine what kind of income you'll need to earn to give you the lifestyle you believe will keep you happy.

✔ Be open-minded and try to come up with alternatives that could save money and not require you to have to earn a greater income.

✔ Explore alternative locations and lifestyle choices that will allow you to live your desired life. Perhaps that would include moving at least part-time to another part of the USA or even to another country. This could have a major impact on how far your money goes.

Chapter 29

YOU CAN GO WHERE YOUR
MONEY GOES MUCH FURTHER

A s the world changes around us, there are more places now available where we can relocate and reside, providing more flexibility than ever. After all, it's really about connectivity. If you have a good internet connection, you can be located just about anywhere. If you can run your business or employment remotely, your options increase exponentially.

More and more of us are looking at alternative locations that allow our dollars to stretch further than they can here in the USA or in similarly priced countries. Although, depending upon where you live in the USA, moving to a state without state income taxes or with a lower cost of living may work as another alternative.

This is a growing trend that is increasing annually. Many retirees are moving to those foreign countries where the quality of life is quite attractive. Some places can be as much as one half of the cost of living as that of a similar quality of life here in the United States.

Large expat communities are growing abroad as more people who are living on social security and meager pensions can barely make ends meet. They hear from or read about others moving to resort-like areas in Mexico, Central, and South America or to European and Asian countries that offer high-quality lifestyles with excellent medical facilities and personnel available. Because of the way the world works with global connectivity, you can keep enjoying your favorite cable shows and network coverage while being able to access local amenities, such as golfing, tennis, gyms, shopping, etc.

These are communities where people can live with others enjoying nice homes and restaurants that rival some of the finest you'll find in the USA. They can be surrounded by natural beauty, friendly people, and welcoming governments who want foreign expats and retirees to relocate to their country.

Some of these countries will give you an opportunity to become a citizen, so you can enjoy citizen benefits such as medical services. That may be available to you by living there for a period of time, purchasing property over a certain dollar limit, or paying the government for a second passport. Some countries offer second passports to those who have a local connection to their immediate family.

There is a monthly magazine called *International Living* that has been around since 1979. It showcases different countries and cities that can be attractive to those considering another or second home as an expat. There are many stories written by those who have moved and followed their dream of living in another country or overseas. Some are quite inspiring and give you a clear insight of what the various countries and cities have to offer. I've been subscribing to it for years and vicariously looking at where it would be attractive to possibly relocate at some point, if not completely, certainly for three to six months out of the year.

As their magazine advertisement states: " . . . *A budget that would have you scrimping and saving at home can, in the right*

places abroad, expand to fund all sorts of comforts—in the Caribbe-
an, Latin America, Southeast Asia, and Europe. On as little as $1,700
to $3,000 a month, a couple in the best-value locales can live quite
comfortably."

Reading the stories and experiences of those who have re-located to some of these places is inviting. They provide a glimpse of what people who relocated went through and how quickly many of them adapted to their new homes. They talk of the friendly, welcoming residents. Some say they wish they had discovered how easy it was to adapt and wish they had done it sooner.

International Living magazine offers updated reports on 24 countries and their locales. They publish an Annual Glob-al Retirement Index on how their top picks rate. They also have courses and publications available for those who want to dive deeper into the subject. Check it out and see for yourself how this could work if you're open-minded about a possible relocation.

I went on vacation to Costa Rica with my family a few years ago. It is such a beautiful country with a highly educated pop-ulation. We found the Costa Ricans very warm, friendly, wel-coming, and hospitable. There were many American expats we spoke with there. Some who have been there for many years. They all seemed to be of the same belief that it was a good move for them. They were enjoying the slower paced lifestyle, and it was much more affordable than the states where they had come from.

There are plenty of other places in the world where you'll hear similar stories. I believe that we'll see more people mov-ing from our American cities and suburbs to some of these countries as time goes on and the cost of living goes up.

ACTION ITEMS

✔ Visit the website www.internationalliving-magazine.
com. Read through it and see if it makes sense for you
to subscribe to their magazine. It is fun and enjoyable
to read about others' experiences moving to different
countries.

✔ Think about how you may be able to relocate and
decide where you may consider moving to. Then do
some research on those locations.

✔ Consider vacationing in the spot where you think it
could make sense for you to move to. Research what
it would cost to live there and whether the lifestyle
would be right for you.

Chapter 30

HOW TO GENERATE INCOME
FROM ANYWHERE

As we discussed earlier, your skillset and services can easily be marketed and used wherever you have an internet connection. In today's world that's just about everywhere. Location is now as interchangeable as the velocity of connectiveness.

Most people couldn't care less where you're located, as long as you can provide the service that they're looking to have rendered. Most of the time your location will not even come up until there's a time zone issue that requires moving your online meeting appointment around.

By exploring some of the freelancer sites I pointed out earlier and comparing fees for services that require skills like your own, you can get an idea of what to charge. You can also find what others are looking for in a service provider and how the marketers are advertising their services.

I'd suggest you post a job just like one you'd be able to do on one of those platforms. This will give you a good idea as to what the competition is offering, how much they're charging and what their qualifications are.

Remember, you'll be seeing people bid on the job from all over the world. It's a very interesting process and enlightening to see how others approach business opportunities from other countries. Having used a few of the websites over the years I will tell you that it's amazing how small our world has become. This process really drives that point home.

Keep in mind that this way of conducting business is becoming more mainstream. You'll see a variety of business providers from the super sophisticated to the most elementary. I know for certain that there's a place for your services out there. People buy people. You're looking for those who resonate with your marketing, language, words, and experience. That's just how the world works.

I have put out bids for graphic design projects, PowerPoint webinar design, editing, audiobook recording, and other projects. I've chosen some based upon their experience and others based upon their sample projects that were sent to me. These weren't chosen only by pricing or location either. Some, I paid higher prices for because they convinced me that their job would be superior.

As you build your resume, references, reviews, and portfolio of sample projects, you'll be able to pick and choose what you want to work on and with whom. There are courses out there that teach you how to optimize your ability to attract business on these platforms.

Skills and services that are in top demand:
- Writing
- Marketing copy writing
- Administrative assistance
- Virtual assistance
- Website design
- PR management
- Technical writing

- Social media management
- Internet research
- Accounting
- Consultancy
- Mystery shopping
- Journalism
- Tutoring

There are many projects available to those willing to put forth the effort to hone their marketing skills in order to find potential money-making opportunities. More freelance skills will emerge as e-commerce gathers greater momentum and better technologies such as artificial intelligence become more sophisticated and popular.

TIP 40: The best way to know which freelance skills are in demand is to stay updated through recruitment portals and the platforms referenced. They carry great listings of freelance jobs and required skills.

Chapter 31

MULTIPLE STREAMS OF INCOME

L et's talk about a concept that is used in a variety of investment circles and methodologies. It's referred to as multiple streams of income. You'll see it referenced in real estate, retail sales, stocks, bonds, currencies, etc. It basically means you receive cash flow from various business ventures or income producing categories.

The ideal set-up is to have several income streams producing cash flow, any one of which can support your lifestyle, or can pay your bills, so you're not stressed about your income. At the very least, these streams can help supplement your retirement income, whether it be social security or pension income, or both.

> *"There is no passion to be found playing small, in settling for a life that is less than the one you are capable of living."*
> - Nelson Mandela

Teeka Tiwari, a super-successful investment advisor and regular contributor in *The Palm Beach Group* investment newsletter understands this. After coming from nothing and having made and lost fortunes, he finally came to this important conclusion and lesson which made all the difference to him for creating wealth:

> "Instead of asking, 'How do I make more money?' which I thought was the solution to all of my problems . . . I started asking myself, 'How do I become wealthy?' That question led me to discovering that big income does not equal wealth. In fact, you can create wealth without ever having a huge income.
>
> What I discovered is, . . . two roads that must be traveled together. The first is to live on a small portion of your income. You must learn how to live below your means. . . . The second road is to secure multiple streams of income. You have to build multiple money machines that spit out cash. Then you have to keep reinvesting that cash and keep doing that for years."

Let's use the example of choosing four or five income streams to create. They can be from your social security, pension, website, online affiliate marketing, or products. In addition, you may have rental income from residential or commercial properties or limited partnership real estate investments. These streams can be from wherever you can create income. There can be as many of them as you like or can handle, but ideally, you want four to five that could each take care of your basic living expenses, ideally, on their own. Sound incredible or too far reaching? It doesn't have to be. Start working on it now and it can come to fruition.

First, you need to determine what your expenses cost you monthly and annually. Then start the process of creating one income stream at a time. Once you get it started and growing, you will be learning the ropes of how to grow an online business, etc.

Once you get the first business up and running, established and growing, you can determine what the next business could be. Keep in mind all this is not going to happen overnight. It takes time to learn how you can do this, but you will get better at it if you put in the time, energy, and focus necessary.

I've met others and know people who have started their on-line business and earn anywhere from a few hundred dollars to tens of thousands a month. The ones who are earning more put a lot of effort initially into getting it going and continue to grow their business. They do this by taking courses and getting coaching from others who are adept and successful at building online businesses.

Perhaps you've heard of the saying from James Allen's *As A Man Thinketh*, "The strength of the effort is the measure of the result." You can apply that to growing your online businesses or any other endeavor you pursue in life.

If you make creating multiple streams of income your ob-jective, develop a plan for creating them, and then execute those plans, it will happen.

In my mind, having this as your financial security plan adds much more security than one or two-income streams. If one or both of those go away, you have a major stressful or ca-lamitous event in your life to deal with.

If you're currently working, you're in a scenario that al-lows you to start the process and prepare for the future before you're in a difficult position.

I know this can work because I have my own income streams that I've created with my books, audiobooks, online courses and coaching and consulting businesses. These can also work cohesively with each other, if that is the way you want to set them up. They can promote the other products in your income streams through different mediums. This can be done through Facebook, YouTube, Google, etc.

You must get started in creating this system for financial independence and protect yourself from uncertain events that can de-rail your livelihood. Tony Robbins has also illus-trated this:

> "There are always two businesses you've got to manage. There's the business you're in, and the business you're becom-ing. If you just manage the business you're in, you're going to get

knocked out by new technology or new competition. But if you're constantly managing those two businesses, you won't have to quit or pivot, because you're always doing something to innovate, or to change, or to improve."

ACTION ITEMS

✔ Create a list of potential income streams that you can create or that you already have and can add to. Brainstorm ideas of how to increase the ones you have, if possible, and pick one you'd like to start growing and building on.

✔ Determine what your living expenses are and what potential income streams could be built to handle some or even all of them.

✔ The important thing is to start the first income stream on the internet. My goal for you is to earn your first dollar from your online business. Once you do that, I know you'll be hooked and want to do more.

Chapter 32

THE OPPORTUNITIES ARE PLENTIFUL

One of my main purposes in writing this book is to highlight and underscore the fact that we are now living in an era that has more opportunities available to us than ever before.

I speak with and hear from many people who are exasperated, frustrated, and discouraged beyond where they ever thought they would find themselves. I can understand why some may feel that way. We've been through and continue to work through difficult times and situations that we have never experienced before.

> "You must not let your life
> play out in the ordinary way.
> Do something nobody else has done.
> Show the world that God's
> creative principle works in you."
> - Paramahansa Yogananda

As I write these words there are those who have figured out exactly what they needed to do to turn things around for themselves. They have made up their minds that *where there's a will, there's a way.*

As mentioned earlier in the book, energy flows where focus goes. You need to decide where you will expend your energy. If it is spent on working on turning things around, it will inevitably do that.

If you haven't considered starting some type of internet-related business, you are living in the past or simply refusing to pay attention to the present. There are so many ways that you can participate in the revenue stream that flows through the internet. It's imperative that you dip your bucket into the multi-trillion-dollar river of commerce to get your share. Don't go down there with a teaspoon. There's plenty to be had if you put forth the effort and learn how to make it work for you. There are so many ways to make money with the internet as a platform, it's hard to know where to start.

There are myriad programs that teach you how to sell on the web. YouTube videos abound on different ways to make money marketing and selling information, products, and services. There are plenty of courses teaching how you can market and sell anything you're looking to make money with on the internet.

You can use online marketing to develop whatever business you've been involved with or want to begin generating income from. It is only limited by your imagination. The only question is, are you willing to explore and learn how to do it?

In the following chapters, we'll explore a variety of ways you can start generating income off the internet. This will help get your own ideas to start germinating. I urge you to start at your earliest possible opportunity. I promise, once you earn your first dollar from it, you will be convinced and will want to do more with it. How do I know? That's precisely what happened to me and many other folks I've met.

There's a wonderful feeling you get when you turn on your computer or look at your smartphone in the morning and find you've earned money on your products, information, or services while you were sleeping. People from around the world can always gain access to your businesses. The idea is to have it working for you consistently, 24/7.

Once you make part or all of your income this way, you will feel the exhilaration of knowing you now have the freedom to take care of your business anywhere you have access to an internet connection.

The business ideas and opportunities I share in the following pages are not intended to be an exclusive list to choose from. Once you see the possibilities that they offer, you'll hopefully become inspired to explore further and find other opportunities available.

ACTION ITEMS

- ✔ Allow your imagination to work on the many ways you can earn income on the internet.

- ✔ Explore options of what's available for online businesses in categories you have an interest in.

- ✔ Google training videos and courses available on online money-making opportunities to get a feel for what others are doing.

PART TWO

BUSINESS IDEAS FOR THE NEW ECONOMY

Chapter 33

CREATE AN ONLINE COURSE

The online educational course industry has exploded and is fast becoming the way most people want to learn new subjects and skills. Costs for online courses run from $10 on the low end to more than $2000 on the higher end, with many of them priced in between. It's projected that by 2525 the eLearning industry will be at $325 billion USD globally.

Online courses are in demand because they're an easily accessible and flexible way to spend your time learning. For example, people can take them on the weekends or from their mobile devices while commuting, depending upon the complexity of the material and the information being taught.

The course you create can be available 24/7, and the world is your audience. I am amazed when I explore some of the platforms that have courses available on them. One that is very popular is Udemy.com. It offers just about every kind of course imaginable and then some. I have purchased good courses online that were very inexpensive but also others that were very amateurish. For example, one I took about navigating Evernote, the note saving app was taught by a man in a foreign country with a web camera perched over his shoulder while he demonstrated on his laptop some of the more popular tips and uses for the app. I did learn from his course, but I was a bit strained at times understanding his accent, and the lighting and sound quality were less than adequate. However, I did not pay much, so I couldn't really expect a professional-looking video course.

This shows that you don't necessarily have to have a professional and polished look to your course. If you're planning on charging the mid to upper end of the pricing structure, you'll want it to look good and have good quality audio as well. Make sure you have a good microphone if you're using your smartphone or computer. You can get them for under $50 and they make a big difference in sound quality on your videos.

There are many resources to learn how to develop a course. There are books on Amazon, YouTube videos, and yes, courses. I suggest you look through the catalog of courses available on Udemy.com to get a flavor for what's available. Also, if there's a course subject that you're interested in, search the web and look at those.

The great thing about having an online course is that once it is up there, you'll continue to generate income from it. I've seen courses on Udemy.com that have generated over $300,000. Obviously, the subject matter and popularity, as well as competition, will impact how much income you'll generate.

TIP 41: Use your course to create a book or vice versa. Send it to a transcribing service and have them send you the transcript. Then, convert it to an eBook. You can also use it as a marketing platform to generate personal coaching and consulting customers. All of these are income generators that can create residual income.

I've had a couple of online courses up for the past few years. These not only generate income even when I'm sleeping, but I also have obtained coaching and consulting clients from their

viewers. There are many benefits to derive from online courses. It's one of the easiest ways to generate recurring income.

ACTION ITEMS

✔ Put some thought into what kind of online course
you can create. Perhaps it's on a hobby you've
become proficient at or even a skill that other
people struggle with.

✔ Check out online courses that are available to give
you ideas on what's out there and what you may be
able to improve upon.

Chapter 34

BUY AN EXISTING ONLINE BUSINESS

This is a strategy that can save you time when creating a business from scratch. There are many reasons why some entrepreneurs can't make their business work or grow further. They sometimes are great at putting the business together but not so great with the marketing end of it. They get stuck and can't figure out the next moves needed. They can be weak in certain components.

Some business owners have other challenges such as dealing with personal issues, running out of capital, or waning interest so they're ready to move on, retire, etc. There are myriad reasons why business owners give up and move on from their businesses. The important thing is to diligently research the business you're looking at, so you're comfortable with the findings. I suggest you enlist help from a good business accountant and attorney who knows what to look for and how to protect you.

An excellent resource to investigate is *Buy Then Build: How Acquisition Entrepreneurs Outsmart the Startup Game* by Walker Deibel. It's available as a book or audiobook on Amazon. You must do your homework up front *before* you jump in with both feet and lay out your cold hard cash.

Make sure you are ready to move forward and make a deal. This will include having team members you want to help you and making a structured business plan that functions as a matrix to share with your team. You can adjust your plan as needed as you move forward.

If you commit to becoming proficient at marketing, copy writing, and sales, you will be well-equipped to build businesses into profitable ventures if the potential is there and you have the right team behind you.

TIP 42: You must keep in mind your exit strategy before you even purchase the business. That way you'll always have a structure that you're building to sell at some point. You'll need to optimize and automate it as much as possible. Most investors looking to purchase an online business are not looking to buy a job. They want something that requires minimum work on their part. You'll be able to optimize your profit if you can show them how automated it is and how easy it is to generate income from it. That would obviously depend upon the type of business you're looking to purchase.

ACTION ITEMS

- ✔ Start by thinking of the types of businesses you may want to explore.

- ✔ Google online businesses for sale to find those who trade in internet businesses and those websites that offer them.

- ✔ Order the book or audiobook, *Buy Then Build: How Acquisition Entrepreneurs Outsmart the Startup Game* by Walker Deibel. Go through it and familiarize yourself with the process. Then, if you're still interested, get serious about your search and make it happen. Deibel lays it out clearly and makes it easily understandable. He also gives you the benefit of his experiences and mistakes.

Chapter 35

BE A COACH OR CONSULTANT IN YOUR AREA OF EXPERTISE

If you've spent 10 years or more becoming proficient in your area of expertise, chances are there is a market for your knowledge and training abilities. Coaching and consulting have become some of the fastest growing segments of education and help for entrepreneurs. It's now a $40 billion+ a year industry and growing by leaps and bounds.

Part of the reason for that is the general acceptance of coaching and consulting for those looking for specific help with a business or task. There are now coaches and consultants for just about any profession, business, or special requirement. I've hired them myself for specific skills I wanted to learn. It can make a huge difference and save you years of trial and error learning.

Coaching can help turn an entrepreneur into a great leader. Consulting, on the other hand, provides that expertise and assistance businesses and individuals often need when they reach a difficult fork in the road or hurdle to overcome. The lines between coaching and consulting can sometimes become blurred, creating a scenario that is not effective at providing what the client needs.

The key difference between coaches and consultants is the focus. With consulting, the focus is on the problem and the consultant offers up different solutions to address the problem. A consultant is an expert who is there to provide answers based on their analysis of the situation.

In coaching, the focus is on the client and on helping them develop their own ability to solve problems and challenges that emerge. Depending upon their needs and skillsets, you can help them with achieving their objectives and guide them accordingly.

Types of Coaching that are popular:
- Life
- Career
- Business
- Executive
- Wellness
- Performance
- Skills
- Financial

Those who provide coaching to businesses are generally paid more, as companies usually have more to spend on coaching than individuals do.

If you're going to create a profession or career coaching business, it's highly recommended you spend time learning best practices and techniques in order to be of optimal assistance to your clients and show a level of professionalism.

There are plenty of resources that can instruct you in setting up and becoming a sought-after consultant or coach. There are also terrific courses and podcasts to help you learn how to market your services.

ACTION ITEMS

✔ Decide what type of coaching or consulting you're interested in doing.

✔ Brainstorm or mind-map an outline of the possibilities available to you and what your coaching or consulting program might offer and look like.

✔ Explore coaching and consulting businesses that are already up and running for ideas on how yours could operate.

Chapter 36

BE AN INFORMATION RESEARCHER/CONSULTANT

This is another one of those professions that is fast becoming a normal part of business needs. There is so much information available now for us to sift through that many of us have a hard time discerning where to look and what to look for. Those who are proficient in searching through the internet to come up with the pearls of information needed are valuable commodities.

Here are questions you can ask yourself to help determine whether you're the right type for information/research consulting:

- Do you like to read?
- Do you like research?
- Are you a people person?
- Are you a logical thinker?
- Are you organized?
- Are you disciplined?
- Are you self-confident?
- Are you computer-literate?

Most information consultants start their businesses by doing work in fields they already have experience in. People in the legal profession usually start their businesses by doing research for law firms, and those experienced in medicine often start off doing medical research. Some people leave their jobs and start businesses with ex-employers as their first clients as long as they're still on good terms.

One of the attractive things about this business is that you can do it from anywhere you have an internet connection. The fees can be lucrative depending upon the industry and scope of the project. Once you build a client base and following, you will be able to move about and take on projects from wherever you're located and make a nice living.

It's possible for you to become an information/research consultant without any experience in the field by subcontracting work from established consultants. There are many variations of this type of work out there *if* it suits your mindset and skills.

Visit websites for organizations devoted to information professionals. A good one to check out is the Association of Independent Information Professionals. There you can look at a list of AIIP members and the type of work they do. Other organizations like the AIIP have websites that also feature links to their members' sites. A look at the membership lists of those professional organizations and a visit to some of their members' sites will show you what information professionals specialize in.

ACTION ITEMS

✔ Decide if this is something you may have an interest in doing and start your own research process to discover where you may fit in this profession.

✔ There are many resources such as books and websites that are devoted to researchers. Do your own search to find what resonates with you to determine if this can be a viable part-time or full-time option.

Chapter 37

CREATE A MEMBERSHIP WEBSITE

A membership website is a great way to build an income stream and provide continuity of income if you know the proper way to build and maintain it. A membership model is simply how and why people join your organization and what they receive in return.

There are many types of memberships available that satisfy our information needs as well as provide connections and resources for business, hobbies, and personal interests. The list is endless. The key is to create one that you believe in and have a passion for, which will make it easier to relate to your customers. Keep in mind that in order to maintain their interest, you must provide them with information that reflects their interests and expectations. I have joined membership sites that I don't visit often, but I enjoy having access to their information when I need it. That's not the way everyone views it, but I have to believe there are many of us out there who view our memberships in that manner.

Fortunately, there are many software programs and resources to learn how to build a profitable membership site that offers members incentives to become and stay members. The last thing you want is to have them become frustrated and leave because they feel they aren't getting their money's worth from it.

The good news is that if you already have an online business that has captured many email addresses, you have a head start. You already have interested people in your database that you can market to.

The beauty of creating a membership website is that there are many ways to add value for others' interests. Let's use the example of a hobby interest site. You can offer members:

- Guest interviews
- Live webinars
- Courses
- Member perks
- Special discounts on supplies, etc.
- Resources
- Member news
- Forums
- Content archives

TIP 43: Another way your membership site can work is with different tiers, such as Silver, Gold, and Platinum memberships. The Silver offers your basic information and baseline perks. The Gold can offer additional perks and add-ons. The Platinum offers further bonuses, perks, special offers, and email consulting to entice the members who want to have it all and can afford it.

As with any other online business, you want to do your homework and due diligence before making a commitment. There are plenty of membership sites out there to get a good idea of how yours might work.

ACTION ITEMS

✔ Start thinking about what your membership site may look like. Decide based on what kind you'd be interested in joining if you were out there looking for one.

✔ Search for sites that interest you, and see how they're structured. Take the best ones you find and use them as a model to create your own.

Chapter 38

CONTENT CREATOR FOR PROFESSIONALS

The creation of 'content' is one of the greater needs out there for professionals looking for more traction in their businesses through their social media outreach. For those who are not familiar with the term 'content', it is basically the information and supporting evidence or background context provided to those who are seeking information. The content provided could come in the form of articles, interviews of experts in the related field, etc.

Unfortunately, many don't have the time or skillset to create effective content. They know that it's a necessity to do it proficiently and regularly, but it seems almost impossible for some due to their lack of related skills and time constraints.

That's where you can come in and save the day. You will need the skillset to create compelling content, and you should also know how and where to share it, so it will gain attention and action from the end viewers.

If you're already familiar with and have spent time in a profession, that is a great place to start touting and marketing your content creation business. You'll be speaking their language and know where the information you're helping to create for them will be best suited and accepted.

Most professionals know that they should be getting their name out there and letting their prospective clients, customers, or patients learn more about them. You can offer them valuable help, enabling them to articulate their skills and differentiate themselves from their competitors.

I have heard of others earning upwards of $50,000 for increasing their clients' business value by creating a marketing campaign that ramps up their business within a reasonably short period, six to eight months or even sooner. This work will require you to have the knowledge needed to be a proficient copy writer, digital marketer, and sales expert. All of these skills are learnable and are not considered rocket science.

There are many great resources and programs available to help you get up to speed quickly in acquiring the skills you need to be a proficient content creator. You do have to commit to constant and never-ending improvement in these skills if you want to earn top dollar for your services. In other words, you must produce results for your clients.

Once you are adept at creating marketing campaigns that generate results for clients, you will be able to pick and choose which customers you want to work with. You'll also be able to work when you want and as much as you want. The big benefit to winning over your clients with great results is that they'll want you to maintain their marketing programs once they see the benefits. That equates to additional income generated to maintain their digital marketing efforts. As you build your clientele, you'll be able to justify charging more once your previous clients provide you with the metrics of how your help increased the value of their services and business. This is a high earning profession for those willing to learn the essential skills to become effective at it.

There are more businesses out there that only have a website and little to no digital marketing efforts. That's primarily because they aren't aware of how much they could increase their business by putting into place a regular marketing program. The opportunities are wide open for you to build a profitable business helping others with their businesses.

TIP 44: You don't have to be the one implementing the digital marketing of your content. You can sub-contract that out at very reasonable pricing. There are digital marketers who are very good at what they do who reside in other countries and are willing to do the job for much less. If you prefer to hire out, you can be the marketing director.

If you already have some or most of these skills, you can jump-start your business by filling in the gaps of the skills and knowledge that you need. If you enjoy marketing and research, this could be an excellent way to supplement your income, and it even become your main source of earnings.

ACTION ITEMS

✔ Make a list of where you believe you need to increase your knowledge and skills and get started acquiring them. Check out the list of resources in the back of the book.

✔ Go on Guru.com, Freelancer.com, Upwork.com, or other similar sites and research what content creators are charging for their services.

Chapter 39

PODCAST PRODUCER

Podcasts have become the preferred method of gaining specific information on subjects, hobbies, and interests for people's education and entertainment, not only for the Millennials and GenX portion of the population. It's also growing in popularity as one of the Boomer generation's preferred information sources. As of 2020, there are over 1 million podcast shows, with over 16 million avid podcast fans, and those programs and audiences continue to grow.

There are most likely people you have met who have expressed an interest in starting a podcast in one of their hobbies or interests. I can tell you from my own experience with it, you need more than the time to commit; there are also many moving parts to creating a viable podcast that others would want to listen to regularly.

There is a need for those who are knowledgeable about producing a podcast and can take over the responsibilities required in running and producing a regular podcast program. Those who are good at it can be paid a decent salary.

Here's a summary of some of the things that need to happen to make a podcast successful:

- Reach leaders in the industry you're producing the podcast about and bring them on your show.
- Schedule times to record each interview.
- Decide on topics that will resonate with the targeted audience.
- Coordinate with the interviewees.
- Record ad spots and intros/outros that makes the show sound professional.
- Write show notes and blog posts based on each interview.
- Design graphics to complement each episode.
- Publish and promote each episode on the host's website, iTunes, and other podcast platforms.
- Develop relationships with your podcast guests to prepare them for the interview.

Some of these positions can be handled by others. If you are busy enough, you can sub-contract some of the above positions to those who specialize in their respective skills. Businesses that handle most of the tasks required of a podcast show will be growing in demand as podcasts become even more popular.

There is no lack of resources and courses available to those who are interested in learning how to produce a podcast. The list keeps growing daily. The important thing to remember is that you must like being in the industry and dealing with lots of different personalities.

ACTION ITEMS

- ✔ Visit course sites available for a clear idea of what it takes to become a podcast producer.
- ✔ Decide if it is something you may want to pursue as a profession. If so, take a course to see if you can become successful at it.

Chapter 40

DEVELOP A DROP SHIPPING BUSINESS

Drop shipping is when a vendor fulfills orders from a third party to have them shipped directly to the customer. The vendors pass on the sales order to the supplier, who then fulfills the order. The vendor usually pays for the item at a discount by working directly with a manufacturer or wholesaler; their profit comes from the difference in the initial item cost and whatever price they sell it at.

The vendor does not store their own inventory or ship items directly. Instead, they focus on marketing, advertising, and managing their online presence. This is where all the skills we've been discussing in terms of marketing, copy writing, and sales come into play. If you learn to do those proficiently, you'll be in a much better position to reap the profits and benefits of running a drop shipping business.

The best part of this business is that you're not handling the products. Your job is to get them sold and handle any customer issues or complaints that occur. Even this end of the business can be farmed out to a third party. However, that's not advisable when you're first starting out. You want to learn what it is that your clients are having problems with so that you can develop solutions. It's best to stay on top of the customers' issues yourself as long as possible, at least until you need help handling them because your business has grown so much.

Beginner drop shippers need to understand that drop shipping is not just another easy money-making scheme. It is a full-time business that requires dedication, consistency, hard work, and a lot of patience. Only with commitment will you thrive in this business.

Some major reasons people fail are that they're in the wrong niche, lack persistence, lack capital, lack customer demand, use the wrong platform, give bad customer support, have delayed shipping, manage the business inconsistently, lack marketing knowledge and effort, and have unprofessional website design and function.

Like many of the previously suggested businesses, professions and platforms, there are a plethora of courses and websites dedicated to the drop shipping business. Once you find your product or niche, then you must be certain you can continue to find other products that your customer base finds desirable. Otherwise, once the market is saturated, you'll run out of sales and your pipeline will be dry.

Many product suppliers can provide you with what you need to establish and keep your business going. The skill is in picking the right product that is in demand. It's obviously a critical one that you must develop. Some of the demand is created by your marketing, which is why it's such an important skill to develop. The other important factor is staying attuned to what's selling out there or starting to trend upwards.

It's a business that requires hands-on attention in order to keep it running smoothly. The numbers can be very impressive when you hit a winning product with the right marketing campaign. It's not uncommon for people to hit $20K+ per month in revenue.

Like any of the other possible web-based industries dis-cussed, you need to do your homework before you go all in. This is one of those businesses that can pay off in a big way if you're willing to do what it takes to make it a winning game for you.

ACTION ITEMS

✔ Do your due diligence on the industry and what it takes to create a profitable business. Then, decide if it's worth the time and effort it takes for you to develop your own.

✔ If you think it could be for you, then take a course or two to see if it still resonates with you. If so, then start small and work your way up to bigger goals once you develop confidence in your abilities and connections.

Chapter 41

BECOME A TRANSLATOR

Our world and its economies have become more connect-ed than ever before. The better we become at market-ing with the other economies in the world, the bigger our share becomes.

There is a growing need for translators with businesses looking to make inroads or who are already doing ecommerce in other countries.

A primary requirement that must be met by translators is a strong academic background showcasing the study of a for-eign language. The translator must also be able to fulfill the requirements of the market which they are aiming to work in as countries differ in their working permit requirements and conditions.

Languages highest in demand are:

- German
- Arabic
- French
- Dutch
- Spanish

- Japanese
- Russian
- Italian

As the translation and interpretation industry grows, so does the range of services that customers are seeking. If you already provide marketing translation services, for example, why not expand your offering to include video translation or desktop publishing services for those wanting to have their written information, website, or books translated. These are highly regarded by clients looking to translate their marketing materials for use across a range of platforms.

If you're a business meeting interpreter, you could support your clients to deliver networking lunches, presentations, or other events. Often, customers aren't aware of which services they need until they are suggested.

The translation market is predicted to hit $1.5 billion by 2024, according to Global Market Insights. This is good news for translators and translator app makers. The Bureau of Labor Statistics projects a 17% employment growth for translators by 2026 due to this need for businesses to go global.

Technology is having an impact on the translation industry but is not about to eradicate it. Only about 5% of translation needs are being met, leaving a huge opportunity for translators to step in and find work or create related businesses.

ACTION ITEMS

✔ If you are bilingual or multi-lingual, you can capitalize on the growing demand for translators. Especially if you have experience in a field that is expanding around the world, such as a tech-oriented industry. Start networking with people in the industry you're familiar with to see where you can start your new career as a translator.

✔ Explore other businesses that may need translators and offer your services.

✔ Go on the freelance platforms and create a listing for your translator services.

Chapter 42

START AN ONLINE STORE

There are tens of thousands of online stores in existence that specialize in all sorts of products and cater to all types of interests and hobbies, from the sublime to the ridiculous and everything in between.

There are those who have fallen into the false thinking and limitations of belief that Amazon is the sole owner of retail items and products. It may seem that way sometimes, but nothing could be further from the truth.

There are several ways you could create an online store. We covered the Drop Shipping business briefly. That can and does work quite well if that's the way you want to handle it. You may create your own products and sell them or even sell others' products. The products your online store offers could be specific to health, beauty, a sport or hobby, a type of food genre, or any other imaginable line. The sky is the limit for what type of store you could create.

It would be best to sell a product that you're not only knowledgeable and passionate about but that you also believe has a big enough audience to grow.

One way to do that is to start out small and test the marketplace first. This can be done in places where those customers and enthusiasts hang out, like in forums, blogs, websites, membership sites, and Facebook groups.

Create a landing page online that offers products and information regarding what you have to offer to see what kind of interest you generate. You can also pre-sell your products. The sales results will give you some barometer of how many people are interested in what you're offering.

You can take it to the next level by creating a basic website and market your products from there through YouTube and Facebook ads to target your marketing efforts toward a specific audience. You need to be prepared to spend some advertising dollars when you get started with this. This can quickly become expensive.

Consider hiring a digital marketing expert who has handled your product or similar products for other clients in the past. Ask for references and examples of similar marketing campaigns they have carried out.

I've read about and heard of others who have successfully created a nice income stream from their specialized online store. It works the same with these as any other online business. It takes perseverance and tenacity. You can't expect to just build it and have customers come. There's a tremendous amount of market and ad testing necessary to see what works and what doesn't. This is done continuously.

TIP 45: Never stop testing your marketing efforts because you never know what actions will take you to the next level. Many people quit way too early because it takes work to figure this out and find the right combination to unlock the treasure chest.

There is no shortage of resources on the web to learn how to sell online and start your own online store. The tough part will be choosing the ones you want to start with. At the risk of sounding too repetitive, you must learn the fundamentals of being in business online today. You need to become excellent at marketing, copy writing, speaking, and selling, all of which are learnable and pay off exponentially!

ACTION ITEMS

✔ Do a mind mapping session and brainstorm ideas about what you'd like to offer on your website and how you could differentiate yourself from the competition.

✔ Conduct an informal survey with people you know or even strangers that you think may have an interest in your products, and ask them what they'd like to see or buy from the ideal version of the site you're looking to create.

✔ Check out whatever competition is out there selling the products you're interested in selling. Determine if what they are offering is what you had in mind. If not, what else can you offer that would attract the same customers to your online store?

Chapter 43

START A SUBSCRIPTION BOX BUSINESS

A subscription box is a service in which customers sign up to receive treats, surprises, and helpful items they always need at the convenience and recurrence they always want, such as monthly. As a subscription box business owner, you'll have the continuity of recurring monthly income that gives you the ability to grow your business and build brand loyalty.

The earliest subscription box appeared in 2004 called The Sampler. It was a collection of samples from independent craft producers, record labels, and zines. Birchbox launched in 2010, and in less than a year, they had 45,000 members. Everyone was talking about subscription boxes from then on.

There are many companies offering subscription services and boxes. Disney has jumped onto the bandwagon, as has Amazon with over 200 different types of subscription boxes. Between 2014 and 2019, the industry grew by 890% and is still growing by leaps and bounds. By 2023, 75% of all companies that sell direct to consumers will offer some type of subscription-based service.

The beauty of the subscription box business is that there are myriad ways to design and market it. First, you must develop your product genre and your customer experience so that they are hooked on your subscription from the first box they receive. Your subscription not only has to be appealing but affordable and, most importantly, profitable. That requires research on suppliers and a platform that delivers superior customer support and experience.

Fortunately, there are a multitude of suppliers and courses that teach the best practices for subscription box businesses and platforms to run your business smoothly.

What are the different types of subscription boxes? Subscription boxes fall broadly into three categories:

- **Curation (55%)** – A service sends collections of new items for customers to sample and use.
- **Replenishment (32%)** – A service sends replacements of the same types of products.
- **Access (13%):** A service allows members to access perks and discounts on items.

There really is no limit to what you can create with subscription box businesses. The only limit is your imagination. It is critical that you test your market and follow the time-tested winning requirements for running a successful subscription box business.

Here is a sampling of some of the more popular subscription box categories:

- Women's Clothing
- Men's Clothing
- Makeup and Beauty
- Grooming and Shaving
- Meal Kits
- Snacks and Candy
- Coffee and Tea
- Wine, Beer, and Alcohol
- Books

- Dog and Cats
- Baby and Kids
- Tech
- Fitness
- Jewelry, Watches, and Accessories
- DIY, Planner, Stationery, and Stickers
- Flowers
- Contacts and Glasses
- Toothbrush
- Vitamins
- Socks
- Candles
- Music
- Home, Gardening, and Decor
- Tactical and Survival Gear
- Outdoor and Sports

It's always best to start where your interests are and where your disposition drives you. That way you have a built-in enthusiasm for your project and product selection starting out.

ACTION ITEMS

✔ Search the web for various subscription box services to generate ideas. Once you identify one or more that you like, do some research on them. Find out more about what they offer and perhaps even order from one to see how it works and what the experience is like.

✔ If you want to learn more about the industry, start your foundational learning by reading more about it and possibly taking a course.

✔ After you become more comfortable with the business and you want to go to the next steps, start designing and developing your own subscription service, then test market it by developing a landing page.

Chapter 44

START A BOOK EDITING SERVICE

Book editing is a service business that is in big demand and continues to grow. Like many other service businesses, there are plenty of wannabees, and many are less than professional or proficient.

If you love books and are detail-oriented, as well as proficient in grammar and spelling, you may find this to be an excellent income stream producer. You'll have to have more than just a little patience. I believe it takes a certain personality to be good at this. The best ones are good at directing and suggesting without being overly pushy or dominating. I have great respect for good book editors. It is a specialized craft.

While it is not legally required to be an editor, taking a course and becoming certified will increase your skills and lend credibility to your expertise. Consider joining a professional association like The Editorial Freelancers Association (the-efa.org) for the resources they offer.

Most editors are supportive of one another, from what I understand, and even have groups such as the Editor Alliance Facebook group. There, you can find helpful ideas and support from a community of editors for everything from grammar to whatever questions you have or help you may need.

You'll need a good bio and website, and you may want to consider finding a mentor or two. If you want to learn the lay of the land first, perhaps you can find an editorial service or another editor that you can freelance for until you gain confidence in your abilities and learn how to interact with clients.

You'll need to decide what you believe you should specialize in. Some editors are skilled at technical editing, like for training manuals and instruction guides, while others specialize in other types of book editing, such as fiction, non-fiction, business-oriented books, or even children's books.

If you can offer to do more than just editing, for example, uploading the final book to Amazon KDP or any of the other book selling platforms, you will set yourself apart from many editors.

Just remember, everything is difficult before it becomes easy. Give yourself time to become used to the business and be kind to yourself. Everybody starts out from the same place. Nobody starts out as a polished professional. That takes time and patience, as well as perseverance. There are good books, podcasts, and resources available to learn more about the book editing business.

ACTION ITEMS

- ✔ Talk to book editors to learn more about the business and determine whether it seems like something you want to explore in more detail.

- ✔ Search Amazon for books and audiobooks on book editing. Find one or two that provide a clear understanding of the business.

- ✔ Search iTunes for any editing related podcasts that you can learn from. This will give you a good idea of issues editors face and how the business works.

Chapter 45

EVENT PLANNING BUSINESS

Many times, when people need to come together for a special purpose, they hire someone to plan it out. An event planner helps to organize events, making sure they run smoothly and are a success. Depending upon the size of the group, its purpose, and the location of the event, it can be a complex endeavor. That's where an event planner comes in to work their magic.

In today's world, events can be tricky. Many events are conducted online, and others take place in a unique location. Whatever the constraints, an event planner works through those and any obstacles, so the attendees aren't distracted by them. This takes a certain amount of skill and finesse to make it appear seamless.

It can be financially rewarding once you gain a track record and experience. Many event planners start out working for other event planners and then branch out on their own.

Some specialize in certain events, such as weddings, corporate events, conferences, or conventions, and others work a variety of event types. Once you've been involved with event planning, you'll know where your talents and natural leanings are toward a particular type or types of event.

TIP 46: There are courses available to learn what it takes to succeed in the event planning industry. One such course can be found at: www.iapcollege.com/program/event-planner-course. The course teaches you the important skills you'll need as well as how to become an event planner, find an event planning job, start an event planning business, and find clients. They also offer a certificate of completion once you successfully finish the course.

You'll obviously want to be able to handle the stress of being an event planner. If you are not good at organizing, interfacing and communicating well with people, and giving directions and delegating, this may not be for you. But, if you have those skills and you like the satisfaction of coordinating all that it takes to create a successful event, seeing your vison through, and having it run smoothly, this may be the type of work you will enjoy.

If event planning sounds interesting, start the learning process and explore further.

You can make this a home-based business or take it to an office setting once you grow it, hire staff, or run it remotely. Either way, you can begin from your kitchen table and expand from there.

ACTION ITEMS

✔ Check out the event planning books available on Amazon, as well as audiobooks on Audible and iTunes.

✔ Find courses and other event planning resources online.

✔ Check for event planning podcasts on iTunes.

Chapter 46

PERSONAL CONCIERGE SERVICE

A concierge is one who handles daily requests and provides assistance with arrangements for others. This can be a lucrative position with the right clients if you have the skillset. One of the commodities people are willing to pay for is time. It's a big scarcity for many people, but especially for people with money who are busy running their businesses and lives.

You can customize your services to your clientele and individual customers. The services you provide can run from the mundane, like running errands, making travel arrangements, buying gifts, and setting appointments, to making arrangements for out-of-town guests to be entertained, doing internet research, organizing their home and business environments, and everything in between. There are concierge services that offer additional services to their clients as well, such as interior design. You can find other services that you can add onto your service and create a wider business relationship with them.

The more skills and experience you have in your tool kit, the more you can customize your service and target clients accordingly. There is a demand for those personal concierges that can free up busy executives and wealthy movers and shakers.

Some concierge services charge by the hour, but many charge a monthly fee. It depends on the client and their needs. Perhaps you only want to work with those who will agree to a monthly fee. It's your choice, so you can design your business model along those lines.

The cool thing about being a personal concierge is that you'll be working with different clients, some with varying needs, so every day will be different. It helps to be creative and flexible. You will most likely come across a variety of personalities that will require you to go with the flow and learn how to accommodate those peculiar people that make up this great big world.

Should you be near a demographic that has a high number of high net worth people, you can cater to them and their needs. That will require you to be more tuned into that type of clientele and have the mindset and skills that they'll require of a personal concierge. You may even be asked to travel with them in order to be able to continue to provide the services they're accustomed to wherever their destinations are.

TIP 47: If you want to become a personal concierge provider, the *International Concierge and Lifestyle Management* (ICLM) is a good resource for concierge services. The association has a professional database and professional resources for those starting out.

As with any personalized business, there are pros and cons. The pros are minimal up-front investment, corporate contracts, and specialization to your strongest skillsets. Cons include dealing with demanding clients and unpredictable schedules, and depending upon your clientele, it can be economy dependent.

ACTION ITEMS

✔ Start looking into personal concierge services in your area to see what the competition is doing and how much they charge. Do your research and due diligence on the business opportunity and determine if it's right for you.

✔ If you're convinced there is a demand, then begin formulating a business plan and putting together your bio and marketing materials.

Chapter 47

21 IDEAS AND ACTIONS YOU CAN USE TO JUMP-START YOUR LIFE

1. People don't pay for value; they pay for perceived value!
2. Optimize/automate/outsource. Be thinking about how to streamline your life and business.
3. The more you get out of your head, the more clearly you'll think. Your head is for having ideas, not holding them. Make a list of all the things you need to get done, then prioritize them. Decide which items are actionable, and create a list of actions for each one. Then start taking action. Create a "Waiting For" list. For example, information to be provided by a co-worker or client, an answer back on a decision that was to be made, etc.
4. Incorporate a weekly review of all project notes, lists, and "waiting for" lists, in order to monitor progress and keep in mind what needs to be done. (In other words, create a 10,000-foot view of what's going on in your life.)
5. Don't forget your hot spots, life's high-level areas, such as faith, family, finance, fitness, and fun.

6. Don't fall under the influence of 'hopeium' that will induce you to think that an untested marketing idea or prospect will bring positive results.

7. If you can define the problem better than your target customer, they will automatically assume you have a solution.

8. Habituate your message. The more someone hears a message, the more believable it is. This familiarity makes a message appear to be true.

9. By following through with action, confidence in your creative abilities will grow.

10. By setting small goals and checkpoints, the process of taking action becomes less overwhelming and gets the ball rolling.

11. Perfection is the enemy of action. The key is to get something, anything, out there and tweak it later.

12. What is the one thing that you believe is holding you back from reaching your full potential? (Brainstorm that. It may take time to uncover.) What would you have to do to eliminate that and create the life you've always wanted?

13. Change your perspective. Go for a walk or hike and let your mind work on your problems. Staring at a computer for hours is not the way to help you generate new ideas.

14. Relax. Stress won't solve your problems. Usually it makes them worse. Try meditation. It calms your mind and body. It allows you to think more clearly and see various solutions that may possibly work.

15. Let it rest and try again later. Taking a break from your problems is ok. Sometimes a good night's rest will be enough to loosen the grip of your issues and give you a new perspective in the morning. Just don't take too long a break.

16. Create three Lists:
    What do I need to do more of?
    What do I need to start doing?
    What do I need to stop doing?

17. Focus on accomplishing small tasks or projects each day.
18. Avoid distractions!
19. Develop a method of tracking your habits while trying to build them. Transfer a paper clip from one jar to another or something similar.
20. Do things differently. Not the same things differently. In other words, try a new approach, tactic or strategy. Perhaps adapt another way to apply a technique or something from another industry. That is, be innovative.
21. Forget all the reasons that it won't work and believe the one reason that it will.

Chapter 48

BELIEVE

I t's not what we know, but what we do with what we know, that creates progress. You picked up this book with the hope that you would discover information that helps you move forward in your life. Perhaps you are looking to find a solution to your current job situation or looking for a career change. Maybe you want to create a whole new lifestyle, or you just want to turn your life around and get unstuck and be happier in general.

Whatever your intent was when you decided to read this book, you can make it happen. It's up to you to decide what that is. Once you decide, you must determine your plan. Then, implement your plan by getting into *action*.

For those of you who already have a strong faith, you already know that it starts with BELIEF. You must first believe in yourself and believe that God is always there to help you. But you need to ask for God's help. It's possible that your faith and courage muscles are weak and flabby from lack of use. If so, there's no time like the present to start working them out.

Paramahansa Yogananda said:

> "In your divinely surcharged will power is the answer to prayer. When you use that will, you open the way through which your prayers can be answered."

This is super-important! In other words, you must do *your* part while *asking* for help and guidance. He also said:

> "Success doesn't come from the outside; it is in your brain. As soon as you think a right thought, work it! Think and act. Think and act! That is how to develop mind power. Every idea is a little seed, but you have to grow it."
>
> Pray: "I want to do it Father. You must guide me; you must inspire me; you must lead me."

While you're working and planning, pray for God's guidance continuously. *Know* that God is working with you and through you to accomplish your worthy objectives. Don't be discouraged if things aren't proceeding as planned. You don't know what path He is having you follow to get there. It may even be something different than what you were expecting. Just *trust* that it will work out and continue to ask for guidance while working toward your goal.

Yogananda said:

> "When trials come you must strengthen your determination to overcome them. If you steadfastly refuse to give up and you go on continuously trying to materialize success, you will suddenly find that mysterious forces have come to your aid and granted your wish."

He goes on to say:

> "You must first thoroughly believe in your own plans and then let the Infinite work through you. You must do your best, but at the same time FULLY BELIEVE that God is helping you. You must realize the power of your own consciousness."

When you plant a seed in the ground you don't dig it up every few days to see if it's growing. You know and trust that it is. You have faith that a sprout is going to come up out of the ground in due time. It's the same with working your faith muscles.

There are many paths to God. I'm introducing my beliefs and what I have found to be helpful in my life. I truly believe there's more to life than just being born, passing through childhood, then adulthood, while working and even raising a family, growing old, then passing away. Why am I here? For what purpose have I come here? Why must we deal with all these vicissitudes of life?

If you place your faith in the world alone, you will be continuously disillusioned by the twists and turns that inevitably come into your life. Just when you think everything is wonderful, something new comes along to spoil your expectations. Eventually, you will experience health problems, loss of loved ones, financial setbacks, a pandemic, etc. Life's vicissitudes are never-ending and will always be around the corner in some form or fashion.

When you allow God to help you throughout life, you have the Giver of All Gifts guiding you. He's the love behind all love, the friend behind all friends, the nearest of the near, and the dearest of the dear. He is the one certainty in life you can count on. His world is designed to teach us that nothing here is permanent or meant to bring us any lasting happiness except Him. Unless and until we understand this and make Him first, we will continue to deal with the world's ups and downs.

It's like when we get something we wanted badly, and then find out after we've had it a while that it no longer has the same luster or effect it had when we first obtained it. Like the billionaire that gets their first billion, then they want two billion, then five billion. How much do we really need to be happy and satisfied? It's never ending. It is all designed to point us back to God. *All of it.*

I want to share with you a short story about what happened to me when I was a child of nine. I was out on a Saturday morning with a friend riding our bikes. We lived out in the country off a main road. There was a big hill we used to walk our bikes up and then coast down. As we were going downhill, we could see through the trees if any cars were coming down the main road. If there weren't any, we would coast through the stop sign, turn left on the main street toward the street we lived on and turn again to continue to coast downhill to our homes.

One morning, I looked to see if any cars were coming and saw none. So, I continued to race to the bottom of the hill to turn left. However, when I got to the bottom of the hill, I saw a car coming that I hadn't seen and slammed on my brakes, only to slide out in front of it. When the car hit me, I remember sliding over the hood towards the windshield and seeing the panicked look on the driver's face.

The next thing I remember is that every second of my nine years flashed before me as I experienced all that happened during my short life, every scent, sound, emotion, in what seemed like just seconds. Sort of like watching a movie rewind but experiencing each second of it in a flash.

God isn't judging you at the end of your life. He lets you re-experience it, and you get to be the judge of what kind of life you lived; what were your predominant thoughts, intentions, motives, etc. Were you kind, helpful, sincere, and loving towards others? What kind of person were you?

Next, I remember floating upwards in a long foggy tunnel with a very bright light at the end. I can remember thinking that if this was death, this is a beautiful feeling. I didn't want the feeling to end. I had never felt so loved. Then I looked down and saw myself sitting on a curb with a group of people standing around me saying, "Call an ambulance! Call an ambulance!". I was thinking, "Hey, that's me down there!" The next thing I knew I was back in my body staring up at all the people I had seen from above, and hearing them say, "Call an ambulance!"

Fortunately, I was miraculously just badly bruised and shaken up. But the experience I had had haunted me. It was more real than anything I had experienced in my short life and left an indelible impression on me. I kept wondering what it was I went through, trying to make sense out of it.

Then, one day a few years later, I watched a show on television about near death experiences. The host was interviewing different people about their experiences. They all explained essentially the same things that I went through. Witnessing their lives being shown before them in moments, going through a tunnel towards a bright light and a feeling of incredible love surrounding them, and having out-of-body experiences.

Once I heard their stories, I felt like I received the confirmation of my own experience. I have never feared death since then because I know that death is a beautiful experience that everyone goes through. There is no reason to fear it. I consider the experience one of the greatest blessings in my life. I'm so glad and blessed I had it at such a young age.

I share this story because I want you to know, dear reader, that there is absolutely no doubt in my mind that there is a God. The love I felt in that experience was like no other love I ever felt in my lifetime. I have much love in my life through my family, friends, and all my loved ones. I realize it is God loving us through them and us loving them with His love.

The most famous near-death experience that I know of is that of Betty Eadie who wrote the New York Times Bestseller "Embraced By The Light." It has sold millions of copies. You can hear her speak about it on YouTube videos. It's a beautiful account of a near-death experience she had in 1973 after surgery, and it has brought solace to many people.

The message in this book is about what I have experienced in my life, that I know in my heart of hearts, has worked and continues to work for me and others who follow these beliefs. To me, it's about results. I've tested these beliefs and received the confirmation I sought.

I suggest that you do the same to get that depth of belief in your heart and mind because without testing and confirming it, you just have blind faith. It's not the same as your own true belief that you've tested and received your own confirmation of. Then, and *only* then, will you *truly* believe. It's worth every effort you make to obtain that. It's life changing and a metamorphosis of your own perspective on life.

We are all God's children and He loves us all equally. Each of us can have a personal relationship with Him. He knows us better than we know ourselves because He created us. We may seem like fragments in His creation, but we are much more than that. He has everything but our love. He gave us free will. He wants us to give our love freely of our own free will. He tests us to see if we want His gifts more than we want Him. We must learn that it is He who we are truly seeking. We will never truly be satisfied or fulfilled unless and until we establish that personal relationship with Him.

As Jesus said, *"Seek ye first the kingdom of God and all these things shall be added unto you."* All the great saints and sages throughout time have said the same thing. Make God first in your life. Buddha, Moses, Mohammed, and all the major religions teach it.

My message in this book is meant to help others to help themselves. The suggested occupations are just a few ways you can get your 'thought wheels' turning and start thinking about new ways to generate income. There are myriad ways to reinvent yourself and re-engineer your life. The new economy is all about being willing to serve God by serving others. By putting others' interests first, you will put the universal laws into action in your favor for prosperity and happiness.

Once you start the process of believing in yourself and putting yourself outside your comfort zone and into your *stretch* zone, you will see the potential you have and be amazed at the opportunities that will begin to present themselves. You will prove to yourself what that means. You'll be able to not only recognize those opportunities but take advantage of them because you will be more willing to grasp them. That's because you will have been working on yourself and your skillsets to give you the confidence you need to stretch. Your faith and courage muscles will strengthen.

You have much more ability than you even know. That's because you haven't tried nearly as much as you're capable of. This happens mainly because we all have those self-imposed mental limitations and hedges we need to overcome. We need to be comfortable with being *uncomfortable* and allow ourselves to discover our true potential. If you make up your mind that you're willing to do that, you will see for yourself how much potential you have and how far you can go. It's much further than you ever dreamed you could.

Trust in God and in yourself. You can and will prove you are capable of so much more if you allow yourself to make the effort necessary.

You hold the power to change your world. It's up to you to decide what next steps you must take. This information has worked not only for me but countless others. I hope you decide to give it a try and start your new journey. It begins with your first steps and builds from there. It is never too late. This is a short journey we're all on. Life goes by quickly.

This is a transformational time we're living in that requires us to be more willing than ever to make the changes necessary for us to become our best. It has shaken many of us down to the core. It is a pivotal moment in our growth as individuals. Make that decision and seize the opportunity to bring out and manifest the best of yourself.

A large group of people in their nineties were interviewed by psychologists. They were all asked the question, "If you had anything to do over in life, what would you have done differently?" The most common responses they heard were,

"I wish I had spent more time thinking," and *"I wish I had taken more risks in life."* Don't let those be your responses when you reach that age.

I wish you much love and blessings with your next steps. May God bless all your efforts in becoming the best that you can be in your life's journey.

Brian Hennessey

ACKNOWLEDGMENTS

First and foremost, I thank God for all the blessings I have in my life that I am both aware and unaware of, and for all the good that I've received and continue to receive. He is the Giver of All Gifts. We need only to open our eyes and become more conscious to see His hand in all we are given.

I've been fortunate to have many great mentors and teachers in my life. I want to thank all of those who have taught me what I needed to know for my career in commercial real estate. To them I am forever grateful and will continue to do my best to pay it forward by teaching others.

I would also like to thank all those extraordinary teachers, of which there are many, who helped me learn everything I know about the information I share in this book. These teachers have instilled a desire in me to be a lifelong learner.

Lastly, I thank those individuals who helped me with the writing of this book in various ways and stages in its development. Also, all those who were willing to read my manuscript and give me their invaluable feedback, I am grateful beyond measure.

To Michelle White, my book editor and designer, who played a huge role as a collaborator in helping me formulate the final version. To Sophia Fischer, who proofread and shared her ideas and perspectives to help me shape the book's style. To

Susie Schaefer who has helped me to see the true potential of the book and used her talents to make it the best it can be.

And last, but not least, to my beautiful wife, Christy, who has helped to make me the person I am today with her support and unconditional love. Without her, this book would have never come to be.

RESOURCES

Book Recommendations
(Most of these are available as audiobooks on Audible.com)

Autobiography of a Yogi, by Paramahansa Yogananda

The Success Principles, by Jack Canfield

The Aladdin Factor, by Jack Canfield & Mark Victor Hansen

The Five Love Languages: The Secret to Love That Lasts, by Gary Chapman

Vivid Vision, by Cameron Herold

Atomic Habits, by James Clear

Fanatical Prospecting, by Jeb Blount

Eat to Live, by Joel Fuhrman M.D.

The 1-Page Marketing Plan, by Allan Dib

Secrets of Closing the Sale, by Zig Ziglar

The New Geography of Jobs, by Enrico Moretti

Profit First, by Mike Michalowicz

The Alter Ego Effect, by Todd Herman

Verbal Judo, by George Thompson and Jerry B. Jenkins

Building a Story Brand, by Donald Miller

The Surrender Experiment, by Michael A. Singer

The Elements of Style, by William Strunk, Jr.

Rejection Proof, by Jia Jiang

Work Rules! by Laszlo Bock

Idea to Execution, by Ari Meisel & Nick Sonnenberg

The 5 Second Rule, by Mel Robbins
Mind Maps, by Kam Knight
Payoff, by Dan Ariely
Unshakeable, by Tony Robbins
The Life-Changing Magic of Tidying Up, by Marie Kondo
Organize Tomorrow Today, by Jason Selk, Matthew Rudy, and
    Tom Bartow
Sell with a Story, by Paul Smith
Grit, by Angela Duckworth
Deep Work, by Cal Newport
The Now Habit, by Neil Fiore Ph.D.
How to Stay Motivated, by Zig Ziglar
Leap First, by Seth Godin
The War of Art, by Steven Pressfield
Buy Then Build, **by Walker Deibel**

Recommended Websites

Yogananda.org (learn to meditate)
Jackcanfield.com (coaching, courses, resources, etc.)
Audible.com (access to hundreds of thousands of
    audiobooks)
Digitalmarketer.com (courses for copy writing, mar-
    keting, etc.)
Clickfunnels.com (courses, platform for online marketing)
Kartra.com (online marketing platform)
Thechiltonmethod.com (book writing and marketing course
    for authors)
Steveharrison.com (courses, resources, training programs to
    help authors)
Tckpublishing.com (resources, articles, courses to help au-
    thors market, etc.)
Briantracy.com (courses, resources on personal and profes-
    sional development)
Ezinearticles.com (get your articles published, resources,
    forms, etc.)

Toastmasters.org (learn how to speak in public)

Udemy.com (online courses)

Upwork.com (hire freelance help for all your needs or become a freelancer)

Guru.com (hire freelance help for all your needs or become a freelancer)

Freelancer.com (hire freelance help for all your needs or become a freelancer)

Bowker: myidentifiers.com (purchase ISBN numbers for your books, needed to sell online and in stores)

Internationalliving.com (find articles, courses, resources, and more about living overseas)

Authority.pub (course for learning how to write, publish, and market your book)

Acx.com (learn how to create and market your audiobooks for Audible.com)

Beaverbuilder.com (WordPress page builder site)

Samadiyoga.com (online live and recorded classes for beginners and advanced yoga practicioners)

MMWbooks.com (Book Designer and Editor Michelle M. White)

Sophiafischer.com (Book Editor Sophia Fischer, sophiafischer @gmail.com)

Troywhudson.com (Voiceover artist for audiobooks, narration, eLearning, etc., Troy Hudson - One of the best!)

ABOUT THE AUTHOR

A successful coach and consultant, Brian Hennessey is the author of four books and an entrepreneur who has successfully created and runs an online course through Impact Coaching Systems. His passion for sharing his experience and lessons learned is evidenced by helping others to learn how to help themselves.

A 35-year veteran of the commercial real estate industry, Brian Hennessey has managed every aspect of the real estate transaction: from developing acquisition and disposition strategies; to conducting market and feasibility analyses; negotiating and executing sales and leases, as well as multistate portfolio transactions totaling approximately 12 million square feet at values in excess of $2 billion.

Each time Brian learned a new lesson, he logged it in a reference manual he created and incorporated it into his system. This was a major game changer. He became a much more competent and confident investor.

Although the title of his most recent book suggests the information is intended for the 'Boomer' generation and even some Gen 'X'-ers, the content is helpful for anyone who is looking to get *unstuck* in these *transformational* times. The main obstacle for most of us is *"we don't know what we don't know."*

If you've been downsized, rightsized, outsourced, or your pro-fession has been turned upside down, this book is for you.

To learn more about Brian Hennessey, his books, resources and consulting services, visit www.impactcoachingsystems.com.